Urban Geography

AN INTRODUCTORY ANALYSIS

SECOND EDITION

by

JAMES H. JOHNSON

Reader in Geography, University College London

PERGAMON PRESS

OXFORD · NEW YORK · TORONTO

SYDNEY · PARIS · FRANKFURT

U.K.	Pergamon Press Ltd., Headington Hill Hall, Oxford OX3 0BW, England
U.S.A.	Pergamon Press Inc., Maxwell House, Fairview Park, Elmsford, New York 10523, U.S.A.
CANADA	Pergamon of Canada Ltd., P.O. Box 9600, Don Mills M3C 2T9, Ontario, Canada
AUSTRALIA	Pergamon Press (Aust.) Pty. Ltd., 19a Boundary Street, Rushcutters Bay, N.S.W. 2011, Australia
FRANCE	Pergamon Press SARL, 24 rue des Ecoles, 75240 Paris, Cedex 05, France
WEST GERMANY	Pergamon Press GmbH, 6242 Kronberg-Taunus, Pferdstrasse 1, Frankfurt-am-Main, West Germany

First Edition 1967
Reprinted 1968
Reprinted Jan. 1969
Reprinted Nov. 1969
Reprinted 1970
Reprinted 1971
Second Edition 1972
Reprinted 1973
Reprinted 1975
Reprinted 1976

Library of Congress Catalog No. 67–21274

cc

Printed in Great Britain by A. Wheaton & Co., Exeter
0 08 016928 7 (flexicover)
0 08 016927 9 (hardcover)

PERGAMON INTERNATIONAL LIBRARY
of Science, Technology, Engineering and Social Studies
*The 1000-volume original paperback library in aid of education,
industrial training and the enjoyment of leisure*
Publisher: Robert Maxwell, M.C.

Urban Geography

SECOND EDITION

THE PERGAMON TEXTBOOK
INSPECTION COPY SERVICE

An inspection copy of any book published in the Pergamon International Library
will gladly be sent to academic staff without obligation for their consideration for
course adoption or recommendation. Copies may be retained for a period of 60 days
from receipt and returned if not suitable. When a particular title is adopted or
recommended for adoption for class use and the recommendation results in a sale
of 12 or more copies, the inspection copy may be retained with our compliments.
If after examination the lecturer decides that the book is not suitable for adoption
but would like to retain it for his personal library, then a discount of 10% is
allowed on the invoiced price. The Publishers will be pleased to receive suggestions
for revised editions and new titles to be published in this important International
Library.

PERGAMON OXFORD GEOGRAPHIES

General Editor: W. B. FISHER

Other Titles of Interest

CLARKE, J. I.	Population Geography, 2nd Edition
CLARKE, J. I.	Population Geography and the Developing Countries
CLOUT, H. D.	Rural Geography: An Introductory Survey
CLOUT, H. D.	The Geography of Post-war France: A Social and Economic Approach
COOKE, R. U. and JOHNSON, J. H.	Trends in Geography: An Introductory Survey
COPPOCK, J. T. and SEWELL, W. D.	The Spatial Dimensions of Public Policy
McINTOSH, I. G. and MARSHALL, C. B.	The Face of Scotland, 3rd Edition
O'CONNOR, A. M.	The Geography of Tropical African Development
SUNDERLAND, E.	Elements of Human and Social Geography

The terms of our inspection copy service apply to all the above books. Full details of all books listed will gladly be sent upon receipt.

TO JEAN

CONTENTS

vii

LIST OF ILLUSTRATIONS

LIST OF TABLES

EDITOR'S FOREWORD TO THE SERIES

ONE of the more striking trends in education over the past few decades has been the enhanced interest in social and environmental studies. Geography, placed by its nature as a central element in these disciplines, has consequently developed greatly as a school and university subject. Starting perhaps from the personal experiences of the many who were brought involuntarily in the early 1940's to see countries and regions other than their own, sustained by widespread acceptance of man as his own proper study, and now increasingly shaped by the growing interdependence of once-isolated communities, geography at the present time commands far greater interest. As a subject it has acquired closer relevance to everyday life, and in so doing has broadened its scope and strengthened its intellectual basis, arriving at an exacter synthesis of the problems that derive from and are fundamentally linked by the fact of terrain.

The contemporary world, twice as heavily populated as in the 1920's and reasonably certain to double again from present numbers by the end of the century, now confronts problems that require increasingly complex solutions. Many techniques and varied specialist approaches are involved: to take two examples only, town planning is far more than a matter of architecture, economics and engineering, and crop improvements can involve a spectrum of studies that range from climate and soil chemistry to educational systems and politics.

This present series of geography texts attempts to provide compact but apposite studies of current topics both on a world level and on a regional scale. Swiftness of change in modern affairs presents difficulties for the large-scale study prepared over several years in that certain details can become partly obsolete even by time of publication. Moreover, the complexity of conditions already alluded to has tended to inflate the major study in content and volume to a size that makes it difficult for the undergraduate student to possess a wide range of such texts.

University of Durham   W. B. FISHER

PREFACE

URBAN geography has attracted more than its share of academic controversy, but no methodological axe is ground here. Individual geographers have naturally tended to see their own particular interests as the focal point of urban study; but, although I have my own views on this matter, this short book simply attempts to produce some order out of a remarkably diverse and rapidly growing field of study. It has been written with the general reader in mind, but it should also prove useful as a framework for the growing number of undergraduate courses in urban geography.

The writing of a general introduction to urban geography has necessarily demanded the selection and compression of material, and I doubt if any two geographers would agree on what should be included or excluded. Selection has been made more difficult by the manner in which the interests of urban geographers have varied from time to time, almost with the caprice of feminine fashion. I hope that I have at least been able to maintain a sane balance among the various topics which have been explored by urban geographers, and that my readers will remember that over-simplification is an almost inescapable result of compression.

A book of this kind must largely be based upon the work of others, but I have thought it undesirable to encumber the text with an over-elaborate system of footnotes. The names of a number of important contributors to the subject are embodied in the text and their work, along with other major sources, are included in the short lists of selected readings provided at the end of each chapter. Footnotes have only been used to cross-reference different sections of the book, to identify specific quotations and to cite interesting pieces of research, which it would have been confusing to have included in the general reading lists, but which individual readers may care to pursue.

The maps in this volume were drawn in the Department of Geography at University College London. I am most grateful to Messrs. K. Wass and T. Allen for their cartographic advice. My wife has not only helped by reading the first draft of this book and correcting proofs, but by her constant encouragement has made it possible for me to complete the text. I owe her a very considerable debt.

James H. Johnson

University College London
September 1966

PREFACE TO THE SECOND EDITION

THE temptation to expand this short book has been largely resisted in this second edition, but the suggestions for further reading have been revised, some minor corrections have been made and a number of chapters have been modified. I hope that readers will continue to find this book provides a readable introduction to some of the many ramifications of urban geography. Its aim is to stimulate the appetite for reading the research literature rather than to provide a bulky, pre-digested meal sandwiched between two thick covers. It is concerned with the findings rather than the techniques of research, and with the topics that urban geographers have thought to be important over the years, linked together in as coherent a fashion as possible.

James H. Johnson

University College London
September 1971

ACKNOWLEDGEMENTS

THE author wishes to thank the following for permission to redraw illustrations from copyright works:

The British Museum (Natural History) and Professor G. Clark, Fig. 1; Mr. R. Merrifield, Fig. 2; Georg Westermanns Verlag, Fig. 4; The Twentieth Century Fund, Fig. 5; Professor W. Wöhlke and the Bundesanstalt für Landeskunde und Raumforschung Selbtsverlag, Fig. 6; Walter de Gruyter & Co. and the Deutsche Archäologische Institut, Fig. 7; D. Van Nostrand & Co., Figs. 9, 10, 11 and 13; The Brookings Institution, Fig. 14; Professor C. Clark and the Royal Statistical Society, Fig. 17; The Editor, *Geographical Review*, Figs. 18 and 20; University of Lund, Figs. 19, 33 and 36; The Editor, *Annals of the Association of American Geographers*, Fig. 21; Mr. Harald Carter and the University of Wales Press, Fig. 22; The Institute of British Geographers, Figs. 23 and 25; The Editor, *Irish Geography* and Professor J. P. Haughton, Fig. 24; Dr. P. R. O'Dell, Fig. 25; Dr. H. Vivian and the *Revue de Géographie Alpine*, Fig. 26; The Editor, *Economic Geography*, Figs. 27, 42 and 50; Professor W. Isard and the M.I.T. Press, Fig. 29; Her Majesty's Stationery Office, Figs. 32 and 38; Professor Hans Carol, Fig. 33; Professor W. William-Olsson, Fig. 34; Dr. D. Diamond, Fig. 36; Faber & Faber Ltd., Figs. 35, 40 and 41; Miss Josephine P. Reynolds, Fig. 43; Mr. R. Lawton, Fig. 44; Mr. J. E. Martin, Fig. 45; Professor S. Dahl, Fig. 46; Department of City Planning, City of Chicago, Fig. 47; University of Chicago Press, Fig. 48; Professor C. D. Harris, Fig. 49; Dr. Homer Hoyt, Fig. 51; Dr. P. H. Mann, Fig. 52; Professor Akin Mabogunje, Fig. 53.

CHAPTER 1

FACTORS IN URBAN GROWTH

THE growth in the number of people who live in cities and the diffusion of urban life to every part of the habitable world is one of the characteristic features of twentieth-century life. Although there have been towns in some restricted parts of the earth since prehistoric times, the modern situation, in which a substantial part of the population of many parts of the world has become urban dwellers and in which cities increasingly dominate social and economic life, had its origins in western Europe only two centuries ago. Since then few cultures have resisted the trend towards city life and the results that this has had on the organization of society and production. What were the technological, economic and social changes which allowed this development to take place?

In examining the factors promoting urban growth, a distinction must be made between those forces which are encouraging the expansion of modern cities to unprecedented size and those which caused the foundation and spread of cities before the Industrial Revolution. Perhaps it is debatable to go as far as Gideon Sjoberg, who has recognized the "pre-industrial" city as a distinct urban type, all the examples of which have common economic and social traits, regardless of where they are found in place or in time. Yet at least the contrast in size is valid and indicates the existence of two distinct technological situations. The first situation was established when the first prehistoric cities were built; the second followed the technical and economic changes associated with the Industrial Revolution.

It is not easy to produce a clear definition of what constitutes an urban settlement and the usual approach is to define a settlement of a certain size, density of population and structure of occupations as being "urban" (with population living outside such settlements being taken as "rural"). Implicit in the recognition of urban places by easily-observable geographical phenomena is the idea that these physical criteria reflect certain underlying economic and sociological qualities,

1

although in practice the precise limits adopted are usually arbitrary. The only functional definition that appears to be generally agreed and applied is a simple one based on the residence of a substantial proportion of non-rural workers in a nucleated settlement (with agriculture, forestry and, sometimes, fishing being considered distinctively "rural" occupations).

Even such simple definitions break down when international comparisons are attempted, since it is often necessary to fall back upon some arbitrary minimum population size as a cut-off point between rural and urban. Such a practice may be inescapable, but it is of doubtful validity since in many cultural realms nucleated settlements of, say, 2000 people may well contain a high proportion of "non-urban" agriculturalists, although a settlement of this size would be commonly classified as urban in various .censuses. But the idea of choosing a minimum population to define urban conditions at least hints at one important characteristic of a town. Unlike a rural village, an urban settlement is significant enough to have more than a local influence. Not only does its social and economic institutions extend over a wider population than is in daily contact with the town, but it also provides links with similar settlements elsewhere.

The Origin of the First Cities

The precise reasons for the original "invention" of cities—if such a term can be applied to what must have been an extended process—must be sought more in the realms of speculation than deduced from observable facts. Certainly an important early step must have been the development of settled agriculture in which the cultivation of cereals was an important element. Not only did this allow the production of a sufficiently large surplus of storable food, but the higher densities of rural population and the greater intensity of agricultural production which eventually developed also made it easier to assemble the surplus necessary to support an urban population. As a result, a small proportion of the total population could be freed from the cares of actual food production and enabled to live in larger settlements than had ever been found before, thus allowing the concentration of groups of specialist artisans and other non-agricultural workers, who formed an essential element in the first truly urban communities.

It is known that at least by 5500 B.C., and probably considerably earlier, mixed-farming communities living in villages were firmly established in South-East Asia (Fig. 1). During the next 1500 years this way

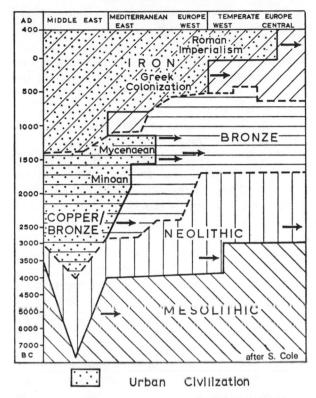

FIG. 1. The diffusion of urban life from the Middle East.
(*Source*: Cole, *The Neolithic Revolution* (1958), p. vi.)

of life spread out from the hills and piedmont areas where it had first matured into the great river valleys of the Middle East. During this period, too, there were certain relevant developments in technology. The ox-drawn plough, the wheeled cart, the sailing boat, and the art of metallurgy were invented. Irrigation techniques were improved and some new crops (in particular the date palm) were also added to the resources of the community. Thus the efficiency of food production was improved and the rivers and estuaries of the alluvial plain provided fish as well as water.

During the millennium after 4000 B.C. some of the villages on the alluvial plains between the Tigris and Euphrates rivers increased in size and changed in function. Cause and effect must have been so intermixed that it would be difficult to sort them out even if specific information were available, yet it is reasonable to suppose that some stimulus must have come from the new environment. Urban settlements in Mesopotamia pre-date the development of large-scale canal irrigation, but even so, the problem of distributing water for cultivation may have encouraged the development of a more sophisticated form of social organization. So, too, may the problem of controlling grazing, since pasture-land was relatively scarce. The alluvial valleys of the great rivers could not be completely self-sufficient, since they were without flints for agricultural implements, substantial building timber, metals and stone. Hence there was an early stimulus for the establishment of trade.

Whatever the precise reason, the villages increasingly became centres for administration, and were used for the exchange, storage and redistribution of goods. Yet it would be wrong to look upon these first beginnings of urban life as a purely economic phenomenon. In the last resort urbanization must have been pre-eminently a social process. Improvements in local transport allowed the food surplus to be assembled in towns, but at the same time new social institutions were necessary to make that food surplus available to urban dwellers. There must also have been profound social changes involved in bringing together larger and more complex communities that became based on collections of specialists of various kinds rather than on self-sufficient family groups. Indeed, the earliest firm archaeological evidence of the changes taking place in these Mesopotamian villages is given by the rise of temples, rather than by any clear indication of economic or technical change. Hence, in this area at least, religious activity may well have been the most important force in bringing non-agricultural communities together and thus setting the processes of urbanization in motion.

The full flowering of independent city states in the Tigris–Euphrates valley came between about 3000 and 2500 B.C., in what archaeologists have called the Early Dynastic Period. Yet there was a limit to the size which these early cities could attain. As bulky food could only be brought from a limited range, and as there may have been as many as 50 to 90 farmers in the total population for every non-agricultural producer, there was a restricted maximum size which any city could reach, given the state of agricultural technology. One estimate puts this limit at 200,000 people, but in fact the actual populations found were much smaller than this. Uruk may have had a population of 50,000 and, later, even the famous city of Babylon probably only reached 80,000 people. Most cities were much smaller than this. These estimates are complicated by the high proportion of agriculturalists who are thought to have lived within the city walls: these may have represented 80 per cent of the population of Early Dynastic cities.

By this time, although priests continued to supervise economic as well as religious activities, an hereditary royal authority had become established. Society seems to have been more clearly divided into social classes, perhaps an indication of increasing specialization of occupations. Certainly at this time there was a great increase in the production of non-agricultural commodities, and trade in some materials took place over considerable distances. For example, copper, used for metal utensils and the decoration of shrines, must have been brought over 1000 miles; and specialized crafts like weaving provided goods for export in exchange for these imports.

Much of the expansion of long-distance trade in valuable articles during this formative period was as much a consequence as a cause of urban growth. The major expansion of specialized crafts came only after these Early Dynastic city states were well advanced, since the possibility of specialization provided by urban life allowed craft techniques to be perfected. Similarly, the problems involved in keeping records and accounts, which were implicit in the new society, provided a powerful stimulus to the invention of writing and to the improvement of skills in mensuration and calculation. Indeed, nearly every culture which has produced elaborate artistic achievements, writing and the beginnings of exact science also shows the development of urban life. It is going too far to say that cities are essential for the arts of civilization, but at least on many occasions they have gone hand in hand.

Urban life may have originated in a number of centres. In indigenous middle America, for example, the city was presumably an independent invention; but the earliest examples of true urban development were found in Mesopotamia, and this centre has had the greatest influence on the development of human society. From here urbanization spread to Ancient Egypt and to the Indus valley; and although specific evidence is often lacking it is also reasonably likely that conditions favourable to the development of urban life were ultimately diffused from this same source into the eastern Mediterranean, inner Asia, China and South-East Asia.

It seems likely that the genesis of urban life in Middle America (perhaps some three millennia later than in the Middle East, but apparently well before European influence had reached the region) was a completely independent development. Yet in spite of differences in time, location and urban form, there were remarkable similarities between the evolving urban societies of both the Old and New Worlds. There was probably a religious stimulus to the development of urban institutions in both areas. The evolution of separate military, religious and political institutions also followed a similar sequence. Both centres of urban genesis, too, had similarities in the organization of trade, tribute and political hegemony. The significance of these parallel developments remains a matter for academic debate, but what emerges clearly is that the genesis of urban life demands a general restructuring of society, both in the growing urban settlements themselves and in the surrounding countryside.

The Extension of Urban Life to Europe

Probably most is known of the extension of urban life into Europe; and this diffusion became the most important strand in urban history, since it was in Europe that many developments took place which were later to transform the geography of cities. The brand of urban life which eventually evolved in western Europe did not hinder the expansion of commerce and industry, and the emigration of population from this region led to the export of city life to many unurbanized parts of the world. The economic success of western Europeans, both in their homeland and in North America, meant that the "Western" city became the dominant urban form in the twentieth century. The historical details of this process cannot be explored here, but a brief summary will emphasize a number of recurring themes of some importance.

During the third millennium B.C. urban life became established in the eastern Mediterranean. Knossos in Crete, Troy in Asia Minor and Mycenae on the Greek mainland, all these and other cities were flourishing during the period. Like the earlier cities of the Middle East, these Mediterranean cities were small and probably had a high proportion of agriculturalists living within them; but one difference lay in the fact that trade was more important in these cities, although the goods involved were still of high value. In this development the highway provided by the Mediterranean must have been very relevant, particularly in the island-studded Aegean Sea, which provided a nursery for sailors before they faced the more intractable problems of the western Mediterranean and beyond. In addition, the skills of craftsmen were developed further in these cities, possibly because of the variety of different peoples who lived around the Aegean, a situation which demanded products intended for an "international" market rather than designed for the tastes of a single society.

At the beginning of the first millennium B.C., cities began to increase greatly in number. In particular, during the eighth and seventh centuries B.C. the Greek city states, which had evolved from the earlier Mycenaean cities, started to hive off daughter settlements, seeking new lands to till, new seas to fish and, not least, new markets to conquer. Given the limited means for transporting bulky food supplies and the physical geography of the eastern Mediterranean, which offered only relatively small patches of cultivable land around each city state, the size attainable by an individual settlement was still limited, hence encouraging this process of migration and colonization.

For example, Cumae, Syracuse and other early colonies in Italy and Sicily were founded from Old Greece between 750 and 700 B.C. In turn, Massilia (on the site of modern Marseilles) was founded from Italy about 600 B.C., and the daughter settlements of this city appeared on the coast of Spain a century later. In this way the Greek city states (and also those founded by the Etruscans and Phoenicians) extended their spheres of influence along the Mediterranean and the pressure of population in the older cities was relieved. By 500 B.C. urban life was found from the Atlantic coast of Spain to the Ganges in India.

During the period of urban colonization a series of technical advances were made, which together represent an impressive addition to the range of human equipment. Iron tools and weapons were developed; alphabetical writing was adopted; the design of ships was improved, so that they could sail more easily against the direction of the wind; and coinage came into more general use in trade. The improved methods of transport and of handling financial transactions encouraged the further expansion of trade. Better iron weapons aided the process of colonization, and more efficient tools, particularly the iron-shod plough, increased the productivity of agriculture. In some city states specialization in craft manufacture and in local agriculture increased, so that long-distance trade in food expanded. Greek cities became increasingly dependent on a limited trade in corn, brought by sea from the shores of Macedonia and the Black Sea.

The impact of this on urban growth is exemplified by Athens of the fifth century B.C. Although to estimate the population of an ancient city is a process fraught with difficulty, it seems likely that Athens possessed at least 100,000 to 150,000 people. Yet although this was a size not encountered before, it must be remembered that most cities at this period still remained much smaller. Often their populations lay between 5000 and 10,000 and they lacked a sufficiently large manufacturing base to make the import of bulky food supplies economically possible.

Improved communications and weapons were indirectly involved in the rise of the Hellenistic and Roman Empires, which themselves provided a further stimulus to urban development both by increasing the number of cities and by encouraging the growth of certain settlements to above average size. About 330 B.C. the unified leadership of the Greeks under Alexander of Macedonia created a new political situation. His conquests rapidly opened up much of western Asia to Greek trade and colonization by absorbing the whole Persian Empire. As a result old cities flourished and new cities were founded. Such factors as a unified currency, new roads, better harbours and larger ships all led to greater trade and hence to general urban development. The responsibilities of empire produced the need for administrators and stimulated the growth of some key cities, like, for example, Alexandria.

Although the Hellenistic Empire dissolved into at least three mon-archies after the death of Alexander in 321 B.C., the stimulus it gave to urban expansion continued: by 100 B.C. Alexandria covered 2200 acres. Regional specialization in agricultural production continued to develop, encouraging both the growth of trade and of cities in those areas where transport by river and sea was available. By the third century B.C. all Greek cities were in need of imported corn, and oil and wine were exported from mainland Greece as far east as Mesopotamia, North Syria, the northern Black Sea and the lower Danube. To the west they reached Carthage, Italy and Sicily. Problems of travel still remained immense. It took longer to cross the Mediterranean by sea than it now does to cross the Atlantic, and with much greater danger. But in com-parison with earlier conditions, movement by sea was more dependable. Land transport within the Empire was also faster and safer, but re-mained almost prohibitively expensive for heavy or bulky goods.

An ever-wider economic and administrative system accompanied the rise of the Roman Empire, which emerged after the Roman defeat of the Greeks in Italy and Sicily. The Carthaginian Empire was also annexed and the former Hellenistic Empire was slowly absorbed. Much of north-west Europe was also brought under Roman rule and influence, for the first time introducing developed urban life north of the Alps. New cities were established in Gaul, in the Rhine valley and in England, although at the margins of the civilized world administration and de-fence were often more important urban functions than trade. Even so, handicraft goods manufactured in these cities found their way beyond the area directly ruled by Rome; and within the frontiers of the Empire the seaways were freed from pirates, roads were built (although it still remained true that food supplies could only be carried relatively short distances by this means), harbours were improved and many towns acquired such essential services as public water supplies.

These developments allowed certain cities to expand greatly in size, if they were both ports and important administrative and trading cen-tres. Population estimates have sometimes erred on the generous side, but even a low estimate puts the population of Rome in the second century A.D. at 200,000 and that of Byzantium during the later Roman Empire at 192,000. Yet most towns were similar in size to those founded by the Greeks. Larger settlements like Roman London covered about 300 acres (Fig. 2), while smaller ones like Caerwent in South Wales measured 44 acres. By analogy with densely built-up modern cities, a town covering 50 acres would have had a population of about 5000, which would mean that Roman London contained some 30,000 people. Hence, except for certain remarkable cities, the earlier limits on urban size still applied, particularly if they were inland settlements and dependent on the food produced in their immediate rural surroundings.

The fall of the Roman Empire in the fifth century A.D. led to a recession in urban life. The stability provided by Roman rule disappeared, trade decreased and cities shrank in size and importance. Many towns in north-west Europe were abandoned; and in Mediterranean Europe urban life survived in very reduced circumstances, with

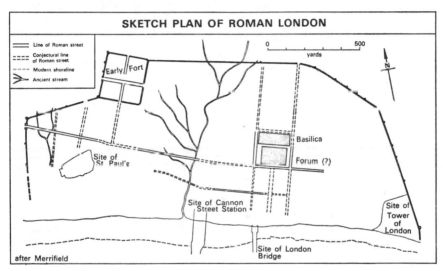

FIG. 2. The size and some features of Roman London. (*Source*: Merrifield, *The Roman City of London* (1965), fig. 30.)

many towns reverting once again to being the foci of small city states. Only in the eastern Mediterranean, in the Byzantine Empire, did urban life continue in its former pattern. In this eastern relict of the Roman Empire larger cities like Alexandria and Byzantium continued to survive, if not to flourish as before.

The Medieval Revival of Urban Growth

The revival of urban life in much of Europe was slow, but by the eleventh century trade was expanding, with the sites of many old Roman towns being rebuilt and entirely new towns founded. Many urban settlements acquired their functions and their administrative distinctiveness only slowly. If conditions were stable some well-placed villages gradually acquired urban functions; or, in more troubled areas, the strongholds of bishops and feudal lords often provided stimuli for urban growth by offering protection to traders and craftsmen. These workers increasingly organized themselves in guilds, which increased their relative importance, so that the history of many towns is largely concerned with the struggle between merchants and feudal princelings, out of which the rights and privileges of the citizens evolved.

In the twelfth century more towns were established with ready-made institutions on sites where no settlement had stood before. An origin of this kind was particularly important where German-speaking settlers were spreading eastwards into central and eastern Europe, but it was also found in western Europe. In North Wales, for example, Caernarvon was founded by Edward I alongside an impregnable castle to strengthen his control of an important location. In south-western France both English and French rulers were active in building *bastides*, as settlements of this kind were called.

Early medieval cities were located at points of greatest accessibility. As local and long-distance trade increased, the urbanized area of Europe was extended, so that, by 1400, the habitable lands of much of western and central Europe were covered with a relatively dense mesh of small towns. Whatever the circumstances of their origin, by this time most towns had acquired basically similar functions. An important proportion of their populations was employed in trade and craft occupations, they possessed legal protection for the rights of their citizens, and they were often centres of local administration and of defence.

The establishment of clearly recognizable towns was found later in areas like Poland, Scandinavia and the Danube lands. In Poland true urban life did not emerge until the middle of the thirteenth century; in Scandinavia many small towns first appeared in the fourteenth and fifteenth centuries; and on the Danube plains occupation by the Turks retarded important urban growth until the eighteenth century.

Medieval Europe was more notable for the rise in the number of towns than for their growth in size. Inland towns demonstrated that the earlier equation between population and local resources remained unaltered, since food supplies continued to be obtained locally. Nuremburg, which may be taken as an example of an important inland medieval town, is estimated to have had a population of 20,000 about 1450. London, with the possible advantage of water transport, reached

40,000 about 1350, probably a similar population to that found in Roman times.

In some locations, however, urban life was re-established in its former glory. Florence in the fourteenth century had 90,000 people, and Venice in 1422 boasted a population of 190,000. Yet estimates of this kind tend to be available only for the more remarkable cities and should not be pressed too far. The population of many towns must have been counted in hundreds rather than in thousands, while even the largest cities had seldom over 50,000 people. During the sixteenth century, however, the population of a few cities began to exceed the level found earlier in Europe; and this change was connected with important economic, social and political developments.

In those areas where commerce was expanding, the old feudal ordering of society decayed and the exercise of power became increasingly associated with the possession and control of money. Hence cities at the crossroads of trade routes were given further encouragement to expand, as merchants became socially and politically more influential. In these areas, too, centralized nations in the modern pattern were evolving, thus stimulating the growth of their capital cities. As national unity was achieved employees of the state increased in number and were often located in the capital; armies were garrisoned there, and the influential few who were seeking political power were attracted to live close to the heart of government. The presence of the court and other leaders of society encouraged the growth of certain craft industries producing luxury goods, and this economic expansion was aided by the focusing of national and international routes on the most important city in the state, particularly as the manufactures produced were often suitable for long-distance, high-value trade.

The associated growth in urban population was often inhibited by the problems of health and sanitation, which were connected with bringing together a substantial population in a limited area. Although this problem was far from solved at this period, some technical advances were made which, if they did not provide a satisfactory urban environment, at least pointed the way for later improvements. In the seventeenth century, for example, a piped water supply was first connected to dwellings in London, and some early steps were made in dealing with the problem of protection against fire.

The rise of nation states also encouraged the extension of urban life to new lands. During the fifteenth century, explorers, aided by an improved compass, pushed out the limits of the known world. Emerging nations like Spain and Portugal, France and England began to acquire colonial empires; with the export of European culture also went the export of urban life. The first colonial towns were little more than ports to exploit the wealth of these colonies or forts to protect the colonists. In the seventeenth century their functions expanded, as permanent settlers developed a richer and more stable life. For example, Williamsburg in Virginia, looking much like an English country town, was laid out in 1633. By the end of the century it was the capital of the new colony of Virginia and could boast the College of William and Mary.

The Impact of the Industrial Revolution

Although the rise of capital cities in Classical antiquity and in Renaissance Europe had produced occasional large cities, the complex technical and economic changes which were the basis of the Industrial Revolution instituted a much more profound alteration in the size of cities, in the proportion of people who lived in them, and in the rate at which urbanization was taking place (Fig. 3). It is sometimes asserted

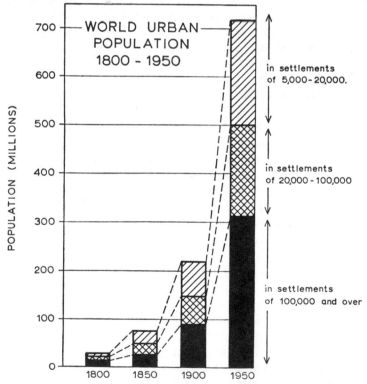

FIG. 3. World urban growth, 1800–1950. (*Source*: Based on statistics in Beaujeu-Garnier and Chabot, *Traité de Géographie Urbaine* (1963), p. 12.)

that these new industrial towns resulted from the larger units of production which were associated with the application of power derived
from fossil fuels to the driving of machinery, hence leading to the need
for larger agglomerations of industrial workers. But this was only one
factor in a whole series of inter-related forces.

Fundamental to urban growth were the great improvements in
agriculture, often linked with a change from subsistence agriculture
to farming aimed almost entirely at production for sale. It is impossible
to date this change precisely: in England, for example, it was taking
place in one form or another from early in the seventeenth century
until the latter part of the nineteenth. For much of this period food
imports from overseas were relatively unimportant and increasing
agricultural productivity was stimulated by the growing demand from
nearby urban dwellers and by the technical ingenuity of some pioneers.

It was within this context that open-fields were enclosed and farms
reorganized, that fenlands were drained and wastelands reclaimed.
New crops were introduced to feed both men and farm animals, the
productivity of livestock breeds was considerably increased, and improved rotations allowed greater yields to be taken from the soil without
loss of fertility. In the same way new implements were invented, and
eventually mechanical power was applied to driving them, hence
increasing the output of the individual agricultural worker. The importance of these developments was not limited to their impact on
food production. The greater productivity of agricultural workers and
the increasing need to count the cost of labour reduced the number of
workers required in agriculture and encouraged many workers to seek
employment in the growing towns, sometimes driven out by conditions
in the countryside, sometimes attracted by better-paid jobs in the towns.

Equally fundamental was the development of improved means of
transportation. The first substantial advance in this field occurred with
the adoption of the canal in late-eighteenth-century Britain. Roads, too,
were improved, primarily for the easier movement of passenger and
mail coaches; but transport by wagons must have benefited also. Such
improvements permitted the location of heavy industry in specialist
towns, since they allowed a much larger market to be tapped by the
new factories and bulky raw materials to be brought in from increasing
distances, both essential prerequisites for the growth of large manufacturing units.

But limits to urban expansion remained. Food was still expensive to
move over long distances and was usually produced in the rural environs
of a city. The larger a city became, the longer were the distances over
which food had to be brought and the more expensive it became. This

tended to inflate money wages and the costs of production in larger urban settlements, thus placing a check on their growth. In addition, the lack of a proper system for the mass movement of people within cities meant that most urban dwellers travelled to work on foot, limiting the size of city which could function efficiently.

The development of the railway and the steamship created a new situation. In Britain a dense network of railways had been established by the end of the 1850's; and one of its earlier effects was to intensify the commercial nature of agriculture in wider areas of the British Isles. In addition, it exposed the countryside more fully to factory-produced goods, reduced the number of rural craftsmen, and thus furthered rural depopulation and the drift of workers to the towns.

This process was carried a stage further in the later 1870's, when grain, grown on the newly-cultivated North American prairies, flooded the British market. The precise economic situation which caused this was a series of poor harvests in Britain, and low freight rates induced by a trade depression; but more fundamental were the developments in the techniques of long-distance transportation, which facilitated the import of cheap food, first from North America and later from Australia, New Zealand and Argentina. Large urban populations could now be fed cheaply and an industrial country was not necessarily limited to home-grown food supplies; for example, in the twentieth century 85 per cent of the population of Britain eventually became urban dwellers. These same developments in transportation increased the effective market for manufactured goods and hence the scale of industrial production. Large cities increasingly became the foci of communication networks which ultimately pushed out into nearly every corner of the world.

A further restriction to the growth of cities was removed with the improvement of internal transport within urban areas, which allowed an increasing separation between place of work and place of residence. In the largest cities the steam railway played a growing role in the internal urban transport system. To the south of London, for example, most railway companies were particularly active from their earliest days in the pursuit of daily season-ticket travellers. Elsewhere in London this form of traffic became increasingly important during the last quarter of the nineteenth century in pushing out the effective limits of the city; and, in addition, the inner sections of the Metropolitan Railway, opened in 1863, pointed to the contribution which underground railways were later to make to travel within inner London.

But road transport was more important in most cities, even the larger ones. Horse buses were found in some European cities from the 1820's, although it was not until the 1870's that their fares became cheap enough to make a substantial impact on travel within cities. In fact, the horse tram was more important in pushing out urban growth along the main highways leading to a city. In Boston, Massachusetts, for example, the limit of dense settlement only extended outwards by about half a mile between 1852 and 1873; but in the fourteen years between 1873 and 1887, encouraged by the opening of new street car routes, development spread 1½ miles further. Then by the end of the century, stimulated in particular by the increasing electrification of the system, the limits of dense urban settlement in Boston were extended another 2 miles.

These changes removed some checks to urban growth and partly explain the fact that throughout the Western world during the last quarter of the nineteenth century cities grew more rapidly than ever before. This expansion was perhaps most remarkable in the United States. Here a close network of railways had been established in the eastern half of the country by the 1870's, and its further elaboration during the rest of the century encouraged the diffusion of urban centres throughout the sub-continent, with large cities being found not only on the sea-coast, on navigable rivers and on the shores of the Great Lakes, but also inland. Existing cities in western Europe also grew rapidly in size. The urban population of England and·Wales doubled between 1871 and 1911, rising from 14 millions to 28 millions. During the same period in France the number of urban dwellers expanded from 11 millions to 17½ millions. And as the cities grew, the positive factors behind their expansion altered in emphasis.

Current Factors behind Urban Growth

One of the most important changes has been in the nature of manufacturing industry. Heavy industries, in which the expense of handling raw materials is a significant element in their costs of production, have become relatively less important. For lighter industries, many of whose products are designed for sale to domestic consumers, the largest cities offer an increasingly attractive location, especially as these cities also provide rapid access to national and international markets. Important, too, are the so-called external economies to be found in large cities. Access to skilled labour, close links with other manufacturers of related products, the availability of ancillary services (such as those provided by advertising agents and wholesalers)—these and similar facilities are more likely to be found in the largest cities and prove attractive to industrialists.

An additional factor encouraging modern urban growth is the increasing proportion of the population of the technically advanced countries employed in tertiary occupations. The tertiary sector of the economy includes a wide diversity of jobs, which involve the provision of services and which, as a result, tend to be found in urban settlements. Partly this change has been associated with rising standards of living, partly with the increasing participation of government in national life, and partly with the increasing number of clerical workers required to service modern industry. The largest urban centres tend to have a larger proportion of tertiary workers because of their greater centrality, which allows their more specialized services to be used more easily. But tertiary activities are found in towns and cities of all sizes; hence the increase in service activities has also stimulated the growth of smaller urban settlements as well as encouraging the extension of the great metropolises.

Social factors, although not always easy to distinguish separately, have also encouraged urban growth. In no sense are these non-economic factors a recent addition to the range of city-building forces, but in the modern world they are particularly influential in encouraging the growth of the largest settlements, particularly if these are capital cities. It is impossible to assess the attraction for permanent residents of a great orchestra, a world-famous art gallery or a unique library, particularly as many of these facilities are also important economically in providing employment and in attracting tourists (and thus indirectly supporting those permanent residents who cater for temporary visitors). But facilities of this kind may also encourage a highly educated *cadre* to live in a particular city; and, as it is from the ranks of these people that key personnel are recruited, their significance in encouraging the location of certain kinds of manufacturing is greatly magnified. For that matter, the attraction of a cultural centre may perhaps lie at a much less sophisticated level, since the snobbish over-tones of living in such a city has an appeal for certain executives (or, perhaps even more strongly, for their wives).

Natural increase of population is another non-economic force which is now playing a more important part in urban growth. Again, this is particularly influential in the largest centres where there is a greater absolute number of people and where, because of recent in-migration, the population contains a higher than average proportion of people of fertile age. Until relatively late in the nineteenth century large urban centres experienced natural decrease—that is, more people died in them than were born there. In Stockholm, for example, until the 1860's the death rate was higher than the birth rate (Fig. 4). Improvement in medical techniques, in sanitation and in the general standard of living has changed this balance, so that large Western cities now show considerable natural increase, often at a rate higher than surrounding rural areas. This has produced a new, but very important, encouragement to urban growth. Thus in south-east England, dominated by the London metropolitan area and its satellite towns, population is expected to grow by 2·4 millions between 1961 and 1981, purely as a result of natural increase. Similarly, the population of the Paris area is increasing

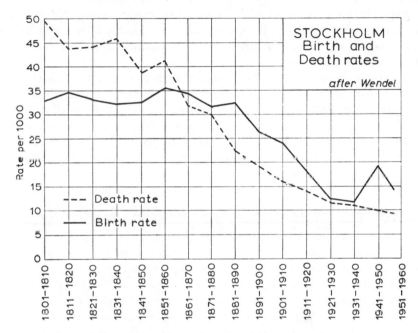

Fig. 4. Stockholm: birth and death rates, 1801–60. (*Source*: Wendel, *Geographische Rundschau* **12** (1960), 249.)

by 60,000 inhabitants a year, not including any immigration from foreign countries or from the rest of France. The demographic factor in the growth of large cities does not end there. Large urban centres, because of their dynamic economies and their existing immigrant populations, attract more than their share of new immigrants, who come from both short and long distances.

The processes encouraging the growth of very large cities have been important since the 1870's and have steadily increased in significance since then. In the twentieth century, however, there have been two further developments which have had important geographical results. These are the development of motor transport and the spread of very large cities to the tropics.

The impact of motor transport on urban form is a theme to which it will be necessary to return later. Here it is sufficient to record that the motor-car and the lorry have encouraged urban dispersal, not only of residential areas, but also of other urban functions, in particular manufacturing industry. As a result, journeys to work can extend over longer distances from large cities, since an increasing proportion of workers do not have to travel right into their central areas. Hence there is an encouragement to the growth of more loosely structured urban areas, which can attain a larger total population than has ever been previously encountered.

The most dramatic actual example of such a situation is found along the north-eastern seaboard of the United States, where there is a continuous stretch of urban and suburban land-use, with a main northeast–southwest axis stretching about 600 miles and a population in 1960 of 37 millions. Here a chain of metropolitan centres, often great ports, has grown together, encouraged by the impact of the motor-car on urban travel and by the dynamic nature of the economies of these cities, which are based on diverse maritime, commercial and industrial functions. Jean Gottmann has called this specific area *Megalopolis* (Fig. 5), although this term was first popularized by Lewis Mumford as a description of any large area of shapeless urban growth.

The second recent development, the spread of large cities to the tropical lands, has been particularly important during the last three decades and especially since the end of the Second World War. In the 1940's, for example, only Bombay, Calcutta, Mexico City and São Paulo among tropical cities had reached a population of more than one million. Now there are at least fifteen cities of this size and their populations are increasing very rapidly. Urban growth is now taking place at a much faster rate in the tropical lands than in western Europe or North America, largely because these areas have considerable leeway to make up. In much of Asia, for example, the rate of urban population growth during this century has far exceeded that of Europe. On the other hand, the level of urbanization (that is, the proportion of the total population which lives in towns or cities) is still much lower than in the Western world. In Asia only 13 per cent of the population lives in cities of over 20,000 people; and in Africa the proportion is as low as 9 per cent. In some of these areas, too, the level of urbanization is increasing only slowly, since the rural population is continuing to expand as well as the urban. Even so, a massive growth in the absolute number of urban dwellers in the developing countries remains a remarkable feature of the human geography of the modern world.

The same forces which encouraged urban growth in the Western world are now beginning to operate elsewhere, but their relative importance is not always identical. An important factor in the growth of very large cities in the tropics is the political awakening of many former colonial territories, with the stimulus which this has for urban growth. Many of these countries still depend on the increasing export

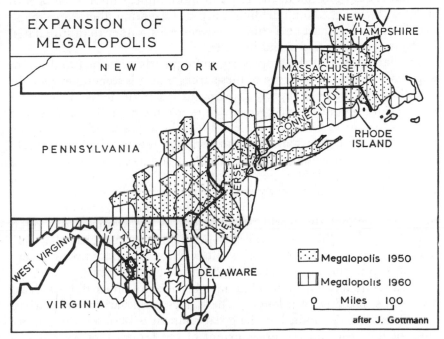

Fɪɢ. 5. The extent and recent expansion of Megalopolis. (*Source*: Gottmann, *Megalopolis* (1961), p. 26.)

of raw materials and the import of manufactured goods: hence many of these "million" cities are ports. Finally, many newly independent countries are encouraging local manufacturing, which, for the same reasons valid in Western countries, tends to be more profitably located in the larger cities, thus furthering their growth.

The expansion of these cities, however, is not always the result of the attraction of urban employment. Even in the underdeveloped countries natural increase is now an important element in the expansion of some cities, particularly as medical treatment is most readily available in urban areas. Although immigration from rural areas still remains the dominant factor in urban growth, even this is partly the result of the "push" administered by the economic state of the countryside rather than of the dynamic attraction of the town. Often the migrants are unskilled and uneducated, so that they form a very poor substratum of urban society, dependent on casual work. In other words, rural–urban migration partly depends on the general economic situation in the under-developed countries, in which the superficial attraction of a small, unreliable cash income in the city has more appeal than a life of subsistence farming, often yielding only a starvation diet. For many people migration must be a choice between evils, rather than stimulated by clear economic and social benefits.

The large cities of the tropics are so frequently discussed and are so important in the urban scene of these areas that it is sometimes thought that they are the only rapidly growing urban settlements. This would not be fully accurate, since growth rates are often similar in towns of all sizes. There is, however, a clear break in importance between the few metropolitan giants and the much smaller towns, which are largely concerned with providing a limited range of services to the surrounding countryside; and similar percentage rates of growth in settlements, which originally differ greatly in size, result in rapidly increasing absolute differences between the small and the large. Like many similar towns throughout the world, small towns in the tropics today often provide a link in the movement of population from rural to urban life, since migration to large cities is often through small towns where migrants from rural areas have failed to find employment.

Urban settlements of some kind have been found on earth for at least 5000 years, possibly even longer. There have been variations in urban forms at various periods, but the great contrast is between the smaller cities of the past and the great extent of the largest modern cities, a phenomenon which is merely 100 years old. Before, even in exceptional cities like Imperial Rome, building was compact and there was always a visible distinction between urban areas and the surrounding country-side. But modern metropolises, which are attracting the greatest absolute increase in population and are steadily dominating the urban geography of the world, are radically different. Even with a motor-car (and perhaps because of it) one often requires hours to travel from the centre to the periphery of these urban giants, and the limits of their built-up areas tend to be increasingly ill-defined.

The growing number of people who live in large cities is one of the most important factors shaping the human geography of the modern world. As nodal points in local, national and international networks of communications they provide vital links for the economic functioning of regions of all sizes. The largest cities provide exceptionally fertile seedbeds for contemporary economic growth. Large cities also create special social environments and, by functioning as centres from which social change is diffused, influence society in areas well beyond their own limits. Similarly, urban areas are centres of political power, with local political influence operating from smaller towns and metropolitan centres dominating national politics. In short, urban settlements provide the context for the changing economic and social life of an increasingly large number of areas. One estimate is that some 18 per cent of the world's population now lives in cities of over 100,000 people, but the dynamic role of urban settlements in the changing economic and social geography of many regions gives cities an importance far greater than their areal extent or even their total populations might suggest.

Selected Reading

Although speculation must play an important part in any interpretation of urban origins, a persuasive, but contested, account is

V. G. CHILDE, The urban revolution, *Town Planning Review* **21** (1950), 3–17. See also his *New Light on the Most Ancient East* (London, 1952).

A broader view of the origin of cities and their diffusion to western Europe is provided by the same author's

What Happened in History (Penguin Books, London, 1948).

Popular accounts which embody more recent archaeological information are

SONIA COLE, *The Neolithic Revolution* (London, 1959); and R. McC. Adams, The origin of cities, *Scientific American* **203**, no. 3 (September 1960), 153–68.

The parallels between urban genesis in early Mesopotamia and pre-Hispanic Mexico are discussed in considerable technical detail in

R. McC. ADAMS, *The Evolution of Urban Society* (Chicago and London 1966).

A general history of urban development and social change is

LEWIS MUMFORD, *The City in History: Its Origins, Its Transformations and Its Prospects* (New York, 1961).

The diffusion of cities in Europe is described in

R. E. DICKINSON, *West European City* (London, 1951).

The agricultural changes which paralleled the industrial revolution are summarized in

C. S. ORWIN, *A History of English Farming* (London, 1949).

For a more detailed study see

J. D. CHAMBERS and G. E. MINGAY, *The Agricultural Revolution, 1750–1880* (London, 1966).

The history of urban growth is discussed in

KINGSLEY DAVIS, The origin and growth of urbanization in the world, *American Journal of Sociology* **60** (1955), 429–37.

The same author brings this statement up to date in

The urbanization of the human population, *Scientific American* **213**, no. 3 (September 1965), 40–54.

A classic account of nineteenth-century urban expansion is

A. F. WEBER, *The Growth of Cities in the Nineteenth Century: a Study in Statistics* (New York, 1899; reprinted Ithica, 1963).

A specialist aspect of nineteenth-century urban growth is discussed in

Centre for urban studies, *Public Health and Urban Growth* (London, 1964).

A more wide-ranging examination of modern urbanization is

P. M. HAUSER and L. F. SCHNORE (eds.), *The Study of Urbanization* (New York, 1965).

See also

J. H. JOHNSON, Urbanization and its implications, *Geoforum* **3** (1970), 7–16.

On the growth of large modern cities see

J. H. SCHULTZE (ed.), *Zum Problem der Weltstadt* (Berlin, 1959).

A more accessible and popular treatment of the same general topic is

P. HALL, *The World Cities* (London, 1966).

"Megalopolis" is studied in

J. GOTTMANN, *Megalopolis: the Urbanized North-eastern Seaboard of the United States* (Cambridge, Mass., 1961).

CHAPTER 2

URBAN SOCIETY AND URBAN FORM

As URBAN life has expanded and been diffused ever more widely, the form which cities have taken at various periods and in different cultural contexts has not remained constant. Hence there is considerable interest in unravelling the contributions which successive technological and social situations have made to the morphology of cities, or to the "town-scape" as some have styled it. Yet, curiously enough, in spite of a long-standing preoccupation among geographers with this theme, few com-prehensive accounts of the visible fabric of individual cities have been written, possibly because of the inherent difficulty of such a task. The difficulty is two-fold: the variety of components which together make up the morphology of an urban area impede its easy description, and the large number of forces which influence that morphology complicate its explanation.

On a map, at least, the most noticeable morphological component is the plan of the streets, which, among other things, may reflect local piecemeal development, past and present means of transport, and chang-ing fashions in what is thought to be an appropriate layout. Once established, the street plan of a particular city is extremely inflexible, partly because of the fixed capital tied up in the streets themselves and in the buildings which face them. It is also inflexible because of the complicated patterns of land-ownership which tend to arise, with the individual parcels of land often tied into the lines of the existing streets. As a result, the street plan produced by a particular group of circum-stances usually survives unaltered, even though it may not be completely appropriate for the changed situation at a later period.

Buildings form another element in the townscape more susceptible to gradual alteration through time, but even a purely utilitarian building will remain for generations. Such a building will be replaced only when it becomes unsafe, or when a clear profit will result from writing off its remaining structural life and replacing it with a new building more suitable for changed conditions. Certain buildings, which are prized for

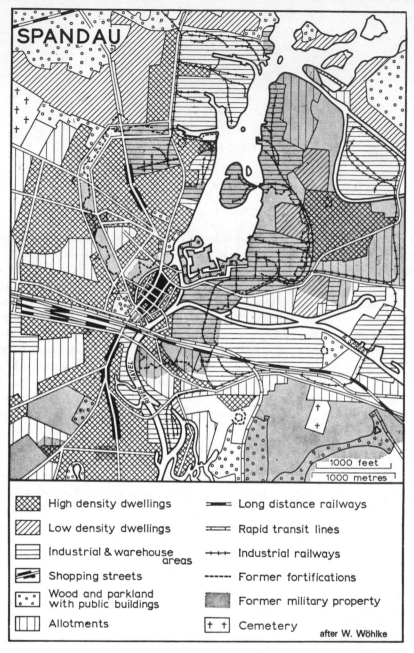

▧	High density dwellings	▰▰▰	Long distance railways
▨	Low density dwellings	▱▱▱	Rapid transit lines
☰	Industrial & warehouse areas	┼┼┼	Industrial railways
⬈	Shopping streets	- - - - -	Former fortifications
⬚	Wood and parkland with public buildings	▦	Former military property
⊞	Allotments	⊹ ⊹	Cemetery

after W. Wöhlke

Fig. 6. Some elements in the urban morphology of Spandau. (*Source*: Wöhlke, *Berichte zür deutschen Landeskunde* **24** (1959), map 1.)

Spandau, on the western fringe of Berlin, provides an example of the detailed complexity which the morphology of an urban area may show. Here urban growth has taken place around a former military area and a shopping centre has developed close to the centre of the old garrison. Rapid suburban rail services have encouraged residential development, and manufacturing industry has grown up in association with facilities for rail and water transport.

their architectural merit, their religious associations or their antiquarian attachments, are likely to survive much longer. Even in a city like New York, where there are remarkably few inhibitions about replacing artifacts from the past, St. Patrick's Cathedral remains on Fifth Avenue, dwarfed by the commercial buildings around it. Yet its religious significance will preserve it indefinitely against the attentions of any property developer.

A third component in the morphology of a city is provided by the functions performed by its streets and buildings (Fig. 6). Function will influence the visible form of buildings most noticeably if they have been expressly designed for their purpose, much more subtly perhaps if a change of use has occurred. But the functions found in a particular area can also be distinguished in other aspects of the townscape, which have a much more ephemeral quality than bricks and mortar. The bustle of people in a city's streets and their activities within its buildings, the nature of the goods sold in groups of shops or distributed by wholesalers, the industrial traffic of a manufacturing quarter—these and similar features are as significant as the form of the permanent structures within an area.

These three strands are woven into the design of the urban pattern. All three tend to change at different speeds and, although they are all closely linked, it is possible for the nature of any individual component to be altered independently of the others. The forces which shape the original form of streets, buildings and functions and subsequent changes made to them are even more diverse, ranging from the nature of technology to the whims of fashion. As a result, all that can be attempted here by way of introduction to this topic is to distinguish some of the themes which have influenced urban morphology at various periods of time and in various social contexts. Although the other components of the townscape will not be completely overlooked, most attention will be given to the urban plan.

The Colonial City

One style of urban plan is associated with cities built where none had stood before. Often this type of city is associated with the occupation of an area for the first time by people with urban life as part of their culture; and this process of colonization produces a particular socio-economic situation which is found in numerous examples, widely spaced in place and in time. In such cities building has to be commenced from scratch and the original settlement tends to possess an over-all plan, rather than be the result of a gradual process of accretion.

Of necessity a pioneering town in a strange place will have a simple plan, which can be easily laid out. In a remarkable number of cases a grid plan, with straight streets set at right angles, has been adopted. Archaeologists have uncovered an example of a grid-plan town from the Indus Valley, where the early city of Mohenjo Daro, dating from about 3000 B.C., was laid out in this form; but a continuous record begins with the Greeks.

When Greek colonial cities were being hived off in the eighth century B.C. the grid plan was commonly adopted. Indeed, this plan is so strongly associated with Greek city building that it was formerly thought that it had been invented by Hippodamos of Miletus, who flourished in the fifth century B.C. In fact, his contribution was to establish a theoretical basis for a plan that had been used earlier and to popularize its use. Miletus, itself the mother city of many Greek daughter settlements, was razed to the ground by the Persians in the fifth century B.C. and was subsequently rebuilt on a grid plan. It prospered further under Roman rule and its area was greatly expanded on the same plan, although a larger size of grid square was favoured for this extension (Fig. 7).

The Romans in turn spread the use of the grid into north-west Europe. The typical Roman camp was laid out in this form, and the same plan was used for permanent Roman settlements in north-west Europe, which had their origin as garrison towns rather than as trading centres. Eventually many of them acquired additional functions, for which the grid plan remained equally suitable. The plans of these Roman towns form a more or less clear nucleus of many modern European cities, in spite of the fact that there has not always been continuity of occupation. Continuity, of course, has encouraged the more complete survival of the original plan. In Turin, for example, the street plan of the city at the end of the sixteenth century exactly reflected the plan of the Roman city. On the other hand, even in the early Middle Ages the Roman plan was difficult to trace exactly in Cologne, although to the discerning eye its influence can still be distinguished.

Medieval towns are often thought of as possessing curiously irregular plans, which resulted from slow, piecemeal growth, but in fact the period was one of great urban colonization, with many towns laid out on regular plans. The square grid was frequently adopted for the thirteenth-century towns associated with the eastward expansion of German-speaking peoples in Europe. The *bastide* towns of south-west France also adopted the grid plan. Thirteenth-century Monpazier, founded by Edward II of England and lying between the Dordogne and the Garonne, provides a fine example of a completely regular plan, arranged around a central market place (Fig. 8).

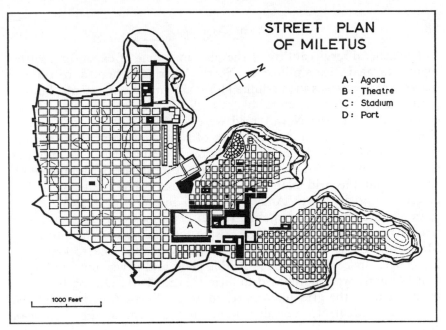

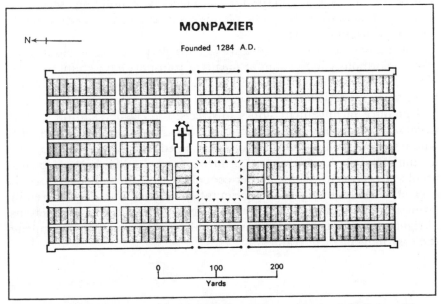

FIG. 7. Street plan of Miletus. (*Source*: Wiegan (ed.), *Milet* . . ., Section 2, vol. 3, Von Gerkan, *Die Stadtmuren* (Berlin), 1935), map 1.)

In its original form Miletus had an irregular form, but after being sacked by the Persians it was rebuilt with a rectangular network of streets. The larger blocks to the south represent a later extension. Form lines are at 5-metre intervals.

FIG. 8. Monpazier: a *bastide* town. (*Source*: Didron, *Annales Archéologiques* **12** (1852), 25.)

The general serviceability of the plan in a time of expanding settlement was again exemplified in North America, where a rectilinear network of streets was soon adopted for many urban settlements. But the plan did not follow inexorably from the fact of colonization. Early Spanish towns in the New World were not built in this form, and in New York the first Dutch settlement of New Amsterdam had a quite irregular street pattern. Yet the tradition of regular urban layouts was such a well-established part of Western culture in the early nineteenth century that the grid plan dominated urban street patterns at this crucial period in North American urban history. In New York, for example, a commission appointed in 1811 proposed a rigid grid-iron street pattern, which formed the basis for the extension of the city along Manhattan Island without any concession to detailed local topography. Little open space was included in this plan, and it was not until 1856 that 840 acres were purchased to form Central Park. During the nineteenth century the grid plan marched across North America with the course of settlement, stamping itself on the form of the American city.

The popularity of this plan for colonial cities in a variety of times and places can be understood by examining its advantages. It is a plan which is easily laid out, even with the services of only slightly skilled surveyors. The plan is particularly suitable if a measured apportionment of land has to be made quickly and efficiently. The plots which it produces are a good shape for the erection of buildings serving a variety of functions. Finally, the plan is easily adapted as a city extends beyond its original limits.

These advantages have not always been perpetuated as cities have grown enormously in size and as means of transport have changed. The obvious disadvantages of the grid plan are found on a site where the topography is particularly broken. Here, if it is rigidly applied, the plan will produce inconvenient slopes to streets, the classic example of this situation in a major city being found in San Francisco. In a large city, where space is at a premium, streets arranged in this way tend to take up unnecessarily large amounts of urban land. In Manhattan, for example, streets occupy some 30 per cent of the total area. The inconvenience of travel at an angle to the orientation of the grid is emphasized in large cities; and, in the era of the motor-car, the numerous intersections at right angles of streets which are roughly equal in importance impede the easy movement of traffic.

The Urge to Build in the Grand Manner

A second example of the role of a particular social situation is the repeated tendency for certain cities to be laid out in what might be called the "grand manner". The most common reason for this style of town plan has been the desire by a ruler to show his affluence and splendour, and, as a result, this kind of morphology is most frequently found in capital cities. The urge to produce a visual expression of worldly power has not been the only factor involved, since the artistic concepts of a particular time and place are also an important influence on the form of city which is erected. Yet at least it can be said that cities in the grand manner are found in a variety of periods and in different cultural contexts.

Imperial Rome, for instance, modified the plan of the typical Mediterranean city, with its relatively small size, its human scale and, in some cases at least, its democratic institutions. Successive emperors of Rome built forums of progressively larger size, and the Circus Maximus and the Colosseum, to name only two examples, represented urban buildings on quite a new scale. Grandeur here was expressed more by the individual buildings than by the plan of the streets, and the application of the grand manner to the street plan of whole cities as well as to buildings can be more clearly seen in the cities of Renaissance Europe, where a number of factors were operating to modify the morphology of towns.

The Renaissance brought the emergence of new nation states, the capital cities of which became a medium for the expression of national power and prestige. Not all states reached the size and influence of France, where national unity was achieved early, but even minor princelings could copy the styles of urban building favoured by absolute monarchs. The Paris of Louis XIV, in which the old walls were removed and new boulevards commenced, is justly famous. But the town of Karlsruhe, founded by Prince Karl Wilhelm of Baden-Durlach in 1715, and planned almost as an appendage to his castle, is inspired by the same motives. Indeed, the plan of Karlsruhe is not far removed from that of Versailles (Figs. 9 and 10).

An important technical change was provided after the fifteenth century by the application of gunpowder to the techniques of warfare. As a result the ramparts and fortifications around towns were greatly elaborated, in order to put as great a distance as possible between a town's buildings and its environs. But more complex fortifications merely represented a transitional stage, because, with improved artillery, these devices were later to lose their effectiveness. In the late eighteenth

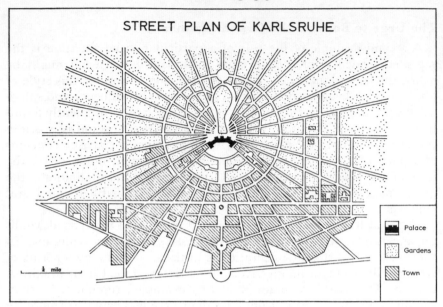

FIG. 9. Street plan of Karlsruhe. (*Source*: Gallion and Eisner, *The Urban Pattern* (1963), p. 46.)

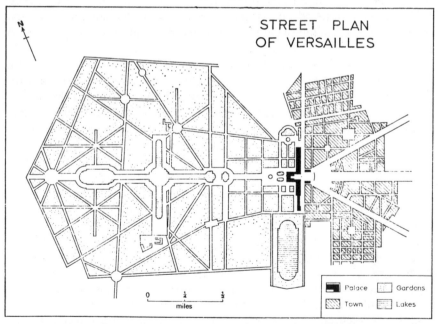

FIG. 10. Street plan of Versailles. (*Source*: Gallion and Eisner, *The Urban Pattern* (1963), p. 46.)

and in the nineteenth centuries the area occupied by the walls and ramparts of many European cities was used for boulevards, public buildings, open spaces, and new speculative building. In the long run gunpowder removed the significance of fortifications in the urban plan and their eventual removal permitted the development of more space-consuming plans.

A further influence was the revolution in the pictorial arts which occurred in Europe about 1400. As well as affecting painting, this development changed ideas of how buildings and streets should be arranged. Perspective took on a new importance, and architects not only erected buildings on a monumental scale, but also became aware of visual techniques which emphasized the scale of their work. The opening up of vistas, which was an important feature in the landscape gardens surrounding great country houses, was equally important in cities. Naturally this was an artistic concept with particular attraction for absolute rulers, since their palaces could be made the cynosure of all eyes. Certainly the creation of vistas influenced the plan of towns from the seventeenth century until at least the end of the nineteenth century.

Paris is a particularly good example of the influence of the grand manner on urban building, since successive monarchs felt obliged to put their stamp on its townscape. Vauban's removal of the old walls of Paris allowed space for the erection of boulevards and promenades to the greater glory of Louis XIV. The massive Place de la Concorde formed part of a considerable extension of Paris to exalt Louis XV. The Paris of Napoleon I was (in the words of Steen Rasmussen) "a new Rome where victories would be celebrated by the erection of triumphal columns and arches".* His Arc de Triomphe completed the great vista along the Champs-Elysées, and the Rue de Rivoli linked the Louvre with the Place de la Concorde. Finally, during the reign of Napoleon III, Baron Haussmann engineered a rebuilding programme of monumental scale. Once again boulevards were carved out of the city and in the open spaces new streets were laid out. Significantly enough, they were also sufficiently wide to prevent the building of barricades.

These various developments brought a radiocentric plan to the streets of many parts of Paris (Fig. 11), but the idea of radial streets was worked out more fully where capital cities were being laid out from first principles. For example, the radiocentric plan was adopted for the new federal capital of the United States, since even though the nation had shorn itself of the trappings of monarchy, it was thought appropriate that national grandeur should be reflected in the plan of Washington.

* S. Rasmussen, *Towns and Buildings* (Liverpool, 1951), p. 142.

The design adopted was by Pierre l'Enfant: diagonal and radial main streets were laid out in the manner being practised in Europe, but they were superimposed upon the grid plan typical of the new American cities. The design perhaps appeared better on paper than it functioned in reality, since this arrangement produced awkward road intersections

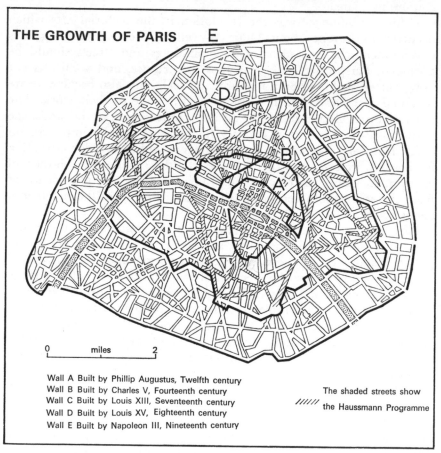

THE GROWTH OF PARIS

Wall A Built by Phillip Augustus, Twelfth century
Wall B Built by Charles V, Fourteenth century
Wall C Built by Louis XIII, Seventeenth century
Wall D Built by Louis XV, Eighteenth century
Wall E Built by Napoleon III, Nineteenth century

The shaded streets show
////// the Haussmann Programme

Fig. 11. The growth and street plan of central Paris. (*Source*: Gallion and Eisner, *The Urban Pattern* (1963), p. 78.)

and building plots which were often difficult to use efficiently. Yet the vistas produced by the radial streets have provided a fine setting for the monumental buildings of the federal government.

The urge to build in the grand manner continues to the present, although the ideas of planning and architecture which shaped earlier examples have been shaken in the twentieth century. As a result the modern expression of this social phenomenon looks radically different, although it is inspired by the same driving force. In the new capital of Brazil, based on a pilot plan by Lucio Costa, travel by motor-car has been kept to the forefront of its builders' minds. Thus in Brasília, as the capital is called, no main roads cross each other on the same level and pedestrians are well segregated from vehicles. Nevertheless it has been thought appropriate to lay out a great axis across the city along which are lined the dramatic modern buildings of the legislature, the presidential palace, the supreme court, the cathedral and various government ministries. Brasília's architecture and planning clearly belong to the second half of the twentieth century, but they elaborate a much more ancient theme.

The Search for an Ideal City

Although most cities have tended to expand in a more or less piecemeal fashion after their original foundation, the idea of designing urban settlements to meet some ideal prescription has a long history. Precepts to guide urban design must have existed for almost as long as cities themselves, but formal plans of ideal cities became common during the Renaissance. At this time there arose the desire, among theoreticians at least, to create cities, not focused on a church or appended to a castle, but offering a well-protected environment for civic life. As a result a considerable number of hypothetical designs were proposed and some, in fact, were implemented.

Two aspects dominated these theoretical schemes. One matter given much attention was the design of improved fortifications. Since the invention of gunpowder simple walls arranged in a square were no longer efficient, and polygonal arrangements were often suggested, with bastions at each corner. It was also necessary to produce street plans which would occupy the area within the walls in the best possible manner. One of the best known of these sixteenth-century urban designers was the Italian, Francesco di Giorgio Martini. His plans were ingenious and technically practical, although the arrangements of streets which he suggested were dominated more by geometrical patterns than by the provision of conveniently shaped building plots.

Palma Nuova provides the best-known example of a theoretical scheme for an ideal city which was converted into reality (Fig. 12). Founded in 1593 in the state of Venice, the town was surrounded by fortifications in the late-sixteenth-century manner. The street pattern, which provided reasonably convenient building plots, was arranged around a central *place*, approached by three highways leading from entrances in the walls.

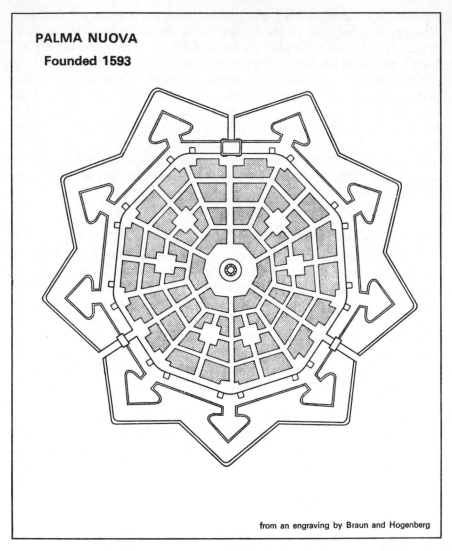

PALMA NUOVA
Founded 1593

from an engraving by Braun and Hogenberg

Fig. 12. Palma Nuova, an ideal city. (*Source*: redrawn and simplified from an engraving in Braun and Hogenberg, *Civitates orbis terrarum* (1599).)

The remaining streets were also arranged in a radiocentric plan, in which six subsidiary squares were set. Similar designs, some of which were carried out, were produced in the seventeenth century.

The altered social and technical situation brought by the Industrial Revolution changed the nature of "ideal" cities and gave them a more utilitarian role. The early result of the industrial changes of the late eighteenth and early nineteenth centuries was to degrade the urban environment, emphasizing such evils as substandard housing, atmospheric pollution and the ill-organized use of land. Not all factory owners, however, were oblivious to the conditions under which their workers lived. Even in the eighteenth century the benevolent paternalism of a few industrialists led them to provide better housing for their employees. Josiah Wedgewood, for example, surrounded his pottery at Etruria with houses of a higher standard of design and convenience than that normally found in the late eighteenth century.

More Utopian ideas, stimulated by a desire to reform society as well as to build better towns, were enshrined in Robert Owen's plan for New Lanark, which he devised in 1816. This factory village was intended to house 1200 people in a co-operative community, with factories and workshops surrounded by a belt of agricultural land. A little-known scheme at Bessbrook in Ireland was much less radical in outlook, but it was equally inspired by a concern for the welfare of an industrial community. In the long run it was more influential since it directly stimulated other practical developments.

Bessbrook was commenced on a site near Newry in 1846 by J. G. Richardson, a Quaker industrialist who laid out a factory village around his linen mill. Although it was not architecturally remarkable, the village was well provided with open space and social amenities. Its importance lies in the fact that Richardson was in touch with Titus Salt and his fellow Quaker George Cadbury. It is probable that the example set by Richardson inspired Salt to build Saltaire, which he commenced in 1852 and which housed some 3000 workers employed in his textile mills. It is even more likely that Bessbrook influenced Cadbury's decision to build his famous town of Bournville, which eventually provided homes for some 2000 families and provided a model for similar towns elsewhere.

The building of Bournville was commenced in 1879; and in 1886 Lever Brothers built Port Sunlight on Merseyside, a low density development with interior gardens and play space for children. Port Sunlight, however, was not the first factory town in nineteenth-century Merseyside, since it was preceded by Bromborough, an almost forgotten village built for the employees of Price's Patent Candle Company in 1853. The idea of a model factory village was continued in Britain at Creswell, a settlement built in 1895 for the employees of Bolsover Colliery. Again, in 1905, the cocoa manufacturer Sir Joseph Rowntree built Earswick near York for his employees; and in 1907 work was commenced on Woodlands Colliery Village, near Doncaster.

The same process was going on independently elsewhere. Pullman, Illinois, was built in 1881 for the employees of the Pullman railway carriage works; Noisel-sur-Seine was built in 1874 by yet another chocolate manufacturer, Menier; Agenta Park, near Delft in Holland, was built in 1883 for the Van Marken Yeast and Spirit Works. All these developments were isolated cases with varying standards of design and execution, but at least these towns were planned with a greater concern for their social implications than that normally found in nineteenth-century industrial areas.

In Britain, at least, the form of these model factory towns reflected other contemporary ideas of the most appropriate mode of urban development, in particular the growing desire to live at lower densities, in detached or semi-detached houses. A tentative history of this theme might begin with the semi-detached houses erected by John Nash early in the nineteenth century in the Park Villages which form part of London's Regent's Park, although Nash in his turn may well have been inspired by the development of the Eyre estate in St. John's Wood about 1810.* These were suburban developments, not complete towns, and they prepared the way for the so-called "garden" suburbs, the first of which was built at Bedford Park in Acton in 1875.

Bedford Park was designed by the famous Victorian architect Norman Shaw and was given a semi-rural, romantic air by its red brick houses, decorated with Dutch gables, casement windows and tiles, and laid out in curved streets with old trees preserved. More famous and more influential was Hampstead Garden Suburb, designed by Barry Parker and Raymond Unwin and begun in 1907. This suburb largely sprang from the enthusiasm of Dame Henrietta Barnett and reflected her ideas of how society should be organized as well as what was considered the appropriate style for residential building. Not only were types of building mixed but, originally at least, the suburb was designed to attract a variety of social classes in houses of different sizes. The suburb was provided with social amenities, making it more than a mere dormitory, although it has no local industry. Its houses were built at an average of eight to the acre, firmly establishing low density housing among the more strongly held tenets of British town planning. It also influenced similar developments in America, Germany and Holland.

Running parallel with the building of garden suburbs was the Garden City movement. The idea of building a garden city was first proposed by Ebenezer Howard in 1898; and it was first realized in Letchworth, built 37 miles north of London and commenced in 1903. Again residential

* For a short account see H. C. Prince, North-West London, 1814–1863, in Coppock and Prince (eds.), *Greater London* (London, 1964), pp. 80–119, especially 100–5.

areas were laid out in a romantic manner and at low densities; but in fact this was quite a different conception, since the houses were set in a self-contained town, with local industrial and commercial areas and the whole urban area surrounded by a belt of agricultural land. In 1919 a second garden city was founded at Welwyn, again lying to the north of London. Although the growth of both towns was slow at first, the thriving communities which exist today indicate the soundness of the original plan for an "ideal" settlement.

The garden cities provided a much larger unit than a typical "company" town, thus reducing the dangers associated with a lack of alternative employment. They were built at a time when the most rapidly expanding industries were being attracted by large centres of population. As a result, it proved possible for them to capture some of the new industries which were being established in the London area, hence ensuring the economic health of the garden cities. The increment in land values which resulted from their growth was retained for the benefit of the community as a whole; and the agricultural belt around the towns maintained their independence from other settlements, at the same time forming a reserve of land for future expansion.

Although representing different basic ideas, the garden cities, the garden suburbs and the late-nineteenth-century factory towns were far from independent of one another. Raymond Unwin was a designer of Letchworth, and also of Hampstead Garden Suburb and Rowntree's Earswick. In their outward appearance at least the garden cities bear a family resemblance to the earlier settlements of Bournville and Port Sunlight; and the industrialists Cadbury and Lever were shareholders in Letchworth. Outside Britain, too, the influence of these three contributions have tended to merge together.

For example, the general idea of "garden" planning influenced the housing provided by the Krupp family for workers in its Essen plant, which eventually provided homes for 16,000 workers. Again, in the United States, the same idea influenced the development of Radburn, New Jersey, which was a suburban community designed by Stein and Wright. This was not a self-contained town, but it elaborated the idea of a garden layout by making its residences face gardens, not streets (Fig. 13). As a result the residential streets became service roads, merely designed to provide rear access to the houses; and the design may be looked upon as a response to the growing impact of the motor-car in the America of the 1930's. The distinctive influence of the garden city movement, however, reasserted itself in Abercrombie's Greater London Plan, in which he proposed the building of New Towns to accommodate part of the overspill population of the Metropolis.

In detail the design of the New Towns shows certain differences from the Garden Cities. For instance, more informal open spaces have been substituted for the formal geometric layout found in the centre of Welwyn; and, as the New Towns were dominated by the need to provide housing for the employees of industries migrating from post-war London,

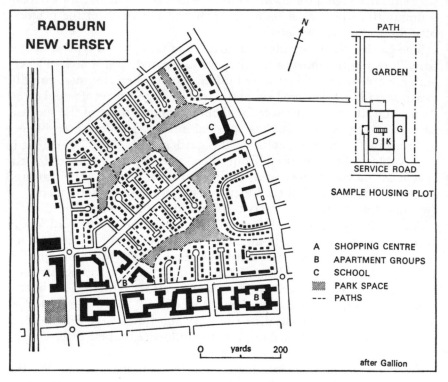

Fig. 13. Radburn, New Jersey. (*Source*: Gallion and Eisner, *The Urban Pattern* (1963), p. 128.)

The "Radburn Plan", as it has become known, was influenced by the growing importance of motor-cars. The houses face gardens, not roads, and are given rear access by short culs-de-sac.

they have become predominantly working-class communities. Yet their debt to the ideas of Ebenezer Howard is clear. Industry has been separated from residence. Housing has been provided at relatively low densities (though not so low as some of the critics of these towns would suggest). Considerable thought has been given to the social implications of urban design, in for example the development of neighbourhood units and in the careful location of schools in relation to residential areas. The 350,000 people who live in the New Towns in the London area, not to mention those who live in similar settlements elsewhere in Britain and abroad, indicate that not all plans for ideal cities fail to make an important impact on the geography of urban areas.

Transport and the Urban Plan

The connection between means of urban transport and the form of cities is many-sided and fundamental. Although the growth and prosperity of cities have always depended on the regional and inter-regional links provided by various forms of transport, it is only relatively recently that the techniques of moving people within cities have put their distinctive mark on their internal form. Before transport within cities became well developed, the centripetal forces operating in urban areas were particularly strong. Most urban dwellers walked to work and the internal movement of goods was difficult. As a result buildings tended to be concentrated in small, compact areas. As techniques of transportation developed, triggered off by the technical inventiveness associated with the industrial revolution, the form of the city also changed. On a broad scale the role of transport in this process can be seen within cities in the relative separation of place of work and place of residence, made possible by the more general adoption of a longer journey to work as part of the daily lives of most urban dwellers.

In the earlier industrial centres, for example, factories were multi-storied, since undue horizontal spread of their operations reduced efficiency. Factory workers lived cheek by jowl with their places of work and, even in homes provided by the most benevolent employers, were housed at very high densities. The members of more prosperous groups also lived in closer proximity to each other than is commonly found in the modern city: the houses of the Bloomsbury squares in London, built in the early nineteenth century for upper middle-class people and their domestic servants, produced higher densities of population than are found in modern local authority housing estates.

In large cities steam railways made important contributions to the developing morphology of urban areas in the nineteenth century. By forging effective links between cities the railway became an important stimulus to urban growth, particularly in the United States; but here it is more relevant to notice its contribution to the detailed form of individual cities. The usual pattern was for railways to link pre-existing settlements to a central city; but sometimes stations were built in the open countryside. Around these stations urban growth would then take place, the rate of growth being related in a general way to the quality of rail services provided and distance of the station (measured in terms of time and cost) from the nearby centre of employment.

In detail, the impact of railway travel on urban growth was influenced by the local situation. The size of the central city was relevant, since railways were most important in the journey to work around the largest cities. The policies of landowners who controlled the sale of land around the new railway stations were influential, sometimes preventing building, sometimes choosing the type of houses it was thought most profitable or most desirable to build. The policies of individual railway companies were equally important in shaping the detailed form of urban development: some companies were not at first anxious to capture local passenger traffic, some wished to carry middle-class commuters, and some, whether through accident or design, were more interested in serving working-class passengers.

Where railway companies were interested from their formative days in serving local passengers, a close mesh of lines was often provided. Stations were located at frequent intervals, and this latter trend was further strengthened by the application of electrical traction to many commuter services in the early twentieth century. The complex system to the south of London is an example of a situation of this kind, since in this sector of London railway companies were unable to attract long-distance freight and passenger traffic, and so turned to short-distance passengers as their main source of revenue. Here urban development around closely spaced stations merged to form what is essentially a ring of continuous building, largely dependent on rail transport for the journey to work. But normally the urban building associated with railway stations, whether located in existing settlements or independent of them, formed distinct nuclei, since most people had to walk to local stations on their way to work.

Even in large cities, however, transport along roads was often much more important than transport by rail. Horse-drawn omnibuses were operating in Paris during the 1820's and in London and New York during the 1830's, but they had less effect than the tram, with its cheaper fares. The impact of trams was greatest in the last quarter of the nineteenth century, when cities were growing in size much more rapidly than ever before. Morphologically the effect of tram and omnibus services was to concentrate urban expansion along the main traffic arteries, producing cities which had a characteristically star-shaped form. In the outer fringes of a typical "street-car" city buildings extended about $\frac{1}{4}$ to $\frac{1}{2}$ mile from the main roads, with interstices of unbuilt land lying between them. Tram services were also important in linking together the built-up areas of groups of closely spaced industrial towns, to form them into loosely grouped conurbations, as, for instance, in West Yorkshire.

Tram and omnibus services had more subtle morphological results than the simple encouragement of urban expansion. By providing cheap transport within cities they allowed many workers to reside for the first time at some distance from their work, thus encouraging the rise of exclusively residential areas. The greater flexibility of movement within cities which resulted from this mechanization of internal travel also stimulated a greater sorting of the homes of particular social groups into distinct districts, although the segregation of classes was not so complete as it was to become in twentieth-century suburbs.

Boston again provides an example: S. B. Warner has described the manner in which social zones developed in this city, following the expansion of the tramway system, which consisted of radial routes linking the centre with the periphery, and cross-town routes linking different sectors of the inner built-up area. Prompted by the pressure of immigrant groups in the more central areas, by the commercial expansion of the city and by the deterioration of older properties, a considerable redistribution of population took place between 1870 and 1890.

Some of the wealthiest inhabitants remained in houses close to the centre, situated in districts of high social prestige; but many built homes on the best sites in the outer suburbs or in outlying dormitory towns. As these people owned private carriages, their location was largely independent of public transport services. The more numerous central middle class, consisting of people like lawyers, successful salesmen and the owners of larger shops, had stable places of work and did not depend on the earning of other members of their families. These people only required to live along a good radial street-car route in the outer suburbs, or close to a railway station offering commuter services. The lower middle class, consisting of office and sales personnel, small shopkeepers and skilled artisans, formed the largest group which could purchase new homes. These people needed to live where there were more flexible tram services, since their places of work often varied from time to time; and even clerks in central offices had busy seasons when they had to get home after working at night or the late evening. In many homes, too, there were a number of wage-earners with a variety of places of work in the one family. As a result the members of this group normally did not live beyond the limits of cross-town street-car services.

The coming of motor buses brought further flexibility to the internal transport systems of cities, but as they also operated on fixed routes their influence on urban form did not differ greatly from that of trams. In the outer suburbs of very large cities, however, buses proved important in allowing building in the gaps between railway stations. In

London, for example, the surface extensions to the underground system made in the 1920's and 1930's would not have tapped enough people to make them economic except for the role of bus services in extending the effective catchment areas of individual stations. Bus services were also important in allowing the daily assembly of the labour forces of the new suburban factories of the period, which themselves were influenced in their location by the growing importance of motor lorries in handling goods.

In the more affluent countries of the world the parallel application of the private motor-car to urban transport has in the long run had much greater significance than the bus (Fig. 14). By using more road space in relation to the number of people moved (to say nothing of the space required for the parking of stationary vehicles) the private motor-car has greatly increased the congestion in the central areas of cities.

UNITED STATES 1940-55
CAR OWNERSHIP AND ECONOMIC GROWTH

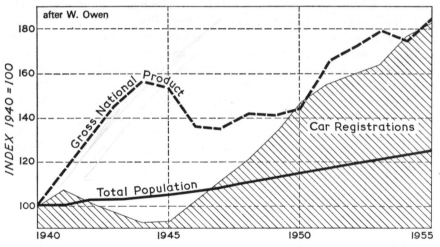

Fig. 14. United States: motor-car ownership and economic growth, 1940–55. (*Source*: Owen, *The Metropolitan Transportation Problem* (2nd edition, 1966), p. 38.)

If the disruption of the Second World War is discounted, the increasing number of motor-cars in the United States can be seen as partly the result of increasing population numbers, but more directly as a product of growing national prosperity.

At the same time, as it is a convenient method of moving people along those main roads where congestion has been overcome by engineering work and also along minor roads which carry a small total traffic, the car has encouraged both the rapid outward extension of cities and infilling between main traffic arteries. With the ease of movement produced by having mechanical transport at one's own front door, it has also been an important factor in encouraging lower densities of residential population.

The morphological results of the motor-car have been greatest in those cities, particularly in the United States, which have experienced all their growth in the twentieth century. If some of the present trends are extrapolated further, the city of the future will be one in which the central area is of steadily decreasing importance and in which suburban shopping centres take an increasingly large share of retail distribution. Similarly, an increasing share of manufacture will be located in suburban industrial estates; and even many of the office functions of city centres will be dispersed. If present trends are continued, the city of the future will be a city cut through by urban motorways with much more space being devoted to road intersections and parking facilities. Its housing densities will be much lower than at present, with the limits of the built-up area becoming more indeterminate, as city workers find that the increased flexibility of transport by car allows them to live just as conveniently in the country as in the town.

Certainly it is clear that a more loosely-structured style of urban area is becoming more generally prevalent. The classic contemporary example is Los Angeles, where freeways have confirmed what was already a dispersed urban pattern. The system of urban motorways in this conurbation has also inhibited the growth of the central business district to the size and dominance which might have been expected, given the total population of the urban area, since many of the functions of central Los Angeles have been decanted elsewhere in the built-up area to other important business centres which can be reached more easily by motor-car.

Dispersed cities of this kind are being duplicated, at least in part, as urban motorways change the internal patterns of accessibility within many other cities. Most American cities now have important suburban shopping centres which have taken some of the functions of the central business district. Usually this process of redistribution has not yet been completed, but many suburban centres are already providing nodes around which other types of employment as well as retailing are clustered. Around them also new residential areas, notable for their more tenuous connections with the central city, are rapidly expanding. In other words, even cities originally focused on one dominant centre are becoming multi-centred in form.

But where new cities are growing from fresh beginnings it is likely that an extremely dispersed urban form will develop, provided that the population is affluent enough to purchase personal road transport and also that low-density residential development is highly valued by society. Flexibility of personal movements will be a feature of the various social and economic activities found in these dispersed cities, provided that road building within them keeps pace with the increasing number of cars. Other morphological changes as well as low density housing will result from this. For example, it will become less and less viable to assess urban structure and population densities in terms of linear distance from the city centre. Instead, generalizations based on the time necessary to travel to a number of centres within the built-up area will be necessary in the future. In addition, certain land uses will be more concentrated on those areas which have local environmental features particularly suitable for them. Certainly one can easily imagine a situation in which sites intrinsically suitable for, say, houses or factories will be developed miles from the rest of the built-up area, with other less suitable sites closer to the central city being left unused for urban purposes.

At least two forces may resist the implementation of this modest prediction. For one thing, strong aesthetic objections, which are now finding expression in the planning law of various countries, have been voiced against the creation of an urban environment of this kind. In particular, attention is being given to regulating the manner in which urban expansion takes place. In Britain, for example, the primary motive in designating a Green Belt around London has been to restrain the expansion of its built-up area. A second restraint lies in the fact that existing cities represent considerable amounts of fixed capital and have their own pattern of vested interests. As a result change tends to be slow, or at least may be channelled into directions which do least harm to existing landowners. One example of this force is seen in the redevelopment of city centres, which is a strong tide in the affairs of the established cities of the Western world. Here an attempt is being made to adapt the central areas of these cities to the demands of motor-cars, at the same time preserving their attractiveness (and land values).

It is perhaps appropriate in conclusion to recall once again that both change and resistance to change are normal features of the urban scene. In any city with a long history an imprint has been left on the urban fabric by the organization and goals of past society and the functioning and economics of past technology. Sometimes those marks are still clear in whole quarters of a city; sometimes there is only a faint trace left in the arrangement of a few streets or in the survival of an individual building. The removal of those features from the past which impede the efficient functioning of a modern city is inevitable and should not be regretted too greatly. Equally, the removal of vestiges of the past should not be undertaken lightly, since it is not inevitable that the contribution of some engineering triumph of the present will appear attractive or useful to future generations. The history of cities and their physical character are irretrievably bound together and to destroy that character unnecessarily is to lose part of an urban heritage.

Selected Reading

The approach of one geographer to the study of urban morphology is provided in

M. R. G. CONZEN, *Alnwick: a Study in Town-plan Analysis* (Institute of British Geographers, Publication no. 17, London, 1960).

A contrasting approach is provided by

E. T. PRINCE, Viterbo: landscape of an Italian city, *Annals of the Association of American Geographers* **54** (1964), 242–75.

An example of the approach of an architectural historian to the same topic is

J. SUMMERSON, *Georgian London* (revised edition, Penguin Books, 1962).

On colonial cities, see

D. STANISLAWSKI, The origin and spread of the grid-pattern town, *Geographical Review* **36** (1946), 105–20.

A good textbook examining the links between urban morphology and the history of planning is

A. B. GALLION and S. EISNER, *The Urban Pattern* (2nd edition, New York, 1963).

A more personal view of the same theme is provided by

S. RASMUSSEN, *Towns and Buildings* (Liverpool, 1951).

An equally personal study of some aspects of the morphology of London is

S. RASMUSSEN, *London, the Unique City* (London, 1937).

A short, well-illustrated description of Brasília is given in

W. HOLFORD, Brasília: the federal capital of Brazil, *Geographical Journal* **128** (1962), 15–18.

The building of "ideal" urban settlements in Britain and the development of the Garden City movement is discussed in

W. ASHWORTH, *The Genesis of Modern British Town Planning* (London, 1954).

See also,

W. L. CREESE, *The Search for Environment—The Garden City, before and after* (New Haven, 1966).

On urban morphology see also the works of MUMFORD and DICKINSON listed after Chapter 1.

On the impact of transport on urban form see

C. CLARK, Transport—maker and breaker of cities, *Town Planning Review* **28** (1957–8), 237–50.

H. W. GILMORE, *Transportation and the Growth of Cities* (Glencoe, Illinois, 1953).

A carefully documented study of the role of one form of transport in shaping urban growth is

S. B. WARNER, *Streetcar Suburbs: the Process of Growth in Boston, 1870–1900* (Cambridge, Mass., 1963).

A similar study for a British city, where there were changing links between the location of industrial plants and housing, is

J. E. VANCE, Jr., Housing the worker: the employment linkage as a force in urban structure, *Economic Geography* **42** (1966), 294–325; Housing the worker; determinative and contingent ties in nineteenth century Birmingham, *Economic Geography* **43** (1967), 95–127.

The effects and implications of the motor-car are summarized in

Traffic in Towns [The Buchanan Report] (London, H.M.S.O., 1963).

CHAPTER 3

DEMOGRAPHIC CHARACTERISTICS OF URBAN POPULATIONS

THE visible landscape of the city is perhaps the most obvious object of geographical study: at least it provides a starting point for the interest of many geographers in urban areas. But associated with the morphology of any city are its past and present populations, which have adhered to certain social and economic institutions, have required to be housed, and have followed distinctive occupations. Even such a crude measure as total population has implications for the importance of a city, since this figure provides a rough indication of the size of the labour force and the nature of the specialized services which a city is likely to offer. Within any city the distribution of population as well as its total has important geographical consequences. In many cities, for instance, there is a logical decrease in the density of population along a traverse from the centre to the periphery, related to the intensity of residential land use.

Within certain urban areas, too, variations in the nature of the population, as well as in its quantity, have put a distinctive stamp on their various internal regions. Some characteristics of the population may be of little relevance in urban geography, since they do not affect the functional organization of the city. The average height of the population and the normal colour of eyes or of hair are examples of variations of this kind. Some characteristics are relevant only in the social and economic context of particular cities: such features as the religious beliefs of different groups in the population and the distribution of ethnic groups often enter into the general functioning of life in a city and may give distinctiveness to various districts within it.

Other characteristics of urban populations, however, are invariably relevant in all cities and at all times. Among the most important of these are the varying demographic structure of the population, measured in terms of its age and sex, and the rate at which population totals are

47

changing. Data on these topics are reliably and frequently collected in most census enumerations; but the interest in this information is inspired by motives other than mere convenience, since the structure and size of the population are the basic biological facts on which the functional organization of any human group is based.

Rural and Urban Contrasts

Possibly the demographic characteristics of urban dwellers which are most stressed are those which distinguish them from rural populations. The precise contrasts which exist depend on the general demographic context, which varies from country to country and time to time. In twentieth-century Western cities, where light manufacturing and service industries form an important sector of their economies, there is normally a somewhat higher proportion of women than in rural areas. For example, in the conurbations of England and Wales there are 102 women to every 100 men. This feature is even more marked among people of working age: in the conurbations of England and Wales there are 105 women between 25 and 44 years old to every 100 men of the same age. Such a situation is not necessarily found in every culture. In the Moslem city, for example, the reverse occurs, because of the different organization of society in which women do not form an important part of the employed labour force. Thus in Lahore, in West Pakistan, there are 775 females to every 1000 males.

Similar contrasts exist between the age structures of urban and rural communities. Urban areas are often centres of in-migration and large cities often provide the greatest attraction for migrants. As a result cities tend to have a smaller proportion of children and older people in their populations, a feature which is most regularly found in larger settlements. If England and Wales are taken as an example, rural districts here possess a higher than average share of people aged 5–24 and, with the smaller towns, have a disproportionate number of older people. On the other hand, the higher proportion of people between 24 and 54 in the conurbations indicates their attraction for people in the prime of their working lives.

A closely related feature is the presence in cities of a larger proportion of the population born outside the local community. The size of this group varies greatly with the unique history of an individual city; and the area which has been tapped for immigrants is connected with the local demand for labour and the nature of society and technology. The early industrial cities of Britain, for instance, drew much of their population from their immediate rural surroundings, but later in the nineteenth century, when railways had made movement easier and greater literacy had led to a wider awareness of available opportunities, workers were tempted to migrate much longer distances, particularly to the larger conurbations.

Or again, if the demand for workers is in the service industries, women are more likely to be attracted than men; if the expanding segment of the urban economy is in heavy industry men will be predominant among the migrants. Among single women migrating to urban employment there is likely to be a greater number of people from a middle-class background; among single men more are likely to be from the working classes. In reality, of course, there is rarely a simple movement of one kind or another. Men and women of a variety of backgrounds move into most growing cities, but the precise mixture varies. The varying social status of the migrants leads them to inner residential areas of varying social desirability, where residential properties, originally built for single families, are now converted to flatlets or boarding houses.

Family groups are also attracted to expanding cities and often these migrants consist of married couples with established families. Indeed, the fact that children are growing up is an important reason for the move of their parents to the city, since not only does urban life offer better prospects for the breadwinner, but it also provides greater social, educational and employment opportunities for his children. These family groups are more attracted by self-contained houses; and as they are likely to have built up some capital, they often move to their own suburban homes. Older married couples are less likely to form part of this movement, since normally an older man is more unwilling to change his job and his children will probably have already begun independent lives of their own.

Not only are there demographic contrasts between rural and urban areas, but there are also differences between various types of city, depending on the functions they perform. Function is important in this context in that it influences the occupational structure of an urban area and hence its likely rate of growth and attraction for different types of worker. For example, H. J. Nelson has shown that between 1940 and 1950 those American cities which he classified as rendering personal and professional services increased at more than double the average rate for the United States. To cite two further instances, the average manufacturing city in the U.S.A. underwent least increase during this period, and cities which were notable as specialist transport centres increased at less than the national average.

Other characteristics of the population of American cities connected with their functions included the proportion of males in the labour force and the average standard of education. In those cities which specialized in providing professional services only a low percentage of men over 14 years old participated in the labour force (55·9 per cent), but on average people living in these cities had spent a higher number of years at school than in other types of city. On the other hand, in manufacturing cities 83 per cent of men over 14 were employed in the labour force (the highest level found in American cities of various functions), but the number of years spent at school was relatively low.

The contrasts due to functional differences among cities were partly masked by general regional variations in population characteristics. The demographic character of the major regions of the United States tended to be impressed on all classes and sizes of cities within them, without obliterating completely the large variations which are produced by different functions. In the west of the U.S.A. there was a general and rapid growth in the population of all classes of city. In this region, also, the proportion of people over 65 was below the national average, the level of unemployment in 1950 was above average, earnings were relatively high and a slightly lower than average proportion of the population participated in the labour force. In contrast, the north-central region of the United States—the area where manufacturing industry was still most important and had been longest established—showed a rate of urban population increase which was lower than the national average. Cities here tended to have a higher proportion of people over 65 years old, but the average income of their populations was above the national average.

Similar regional differences are present in Britain. C. A. Moser and W. Scott, in a study of British towns which will be mentioned later, examined such features as social class, population change and overcrowding in the 157 towns in England and Wales which had a population of 50,000 or more in 1951. Not only did certain specialist towns like resorts and exclusive suburbs stand out as being demographically distinctive, but, very broadly, a contrast between northern and southern England emerged, with urban areas in the north being characterized by a higher proportion of working-class people, less dynamic growth and greater overcrowding.

Internal Population Variations

Not only are there contrasts among the populations of cities with different functions and located in different regions, but there are also contrasts among the various residential areas within individual cities.

The development of distinctive residential areas will be examined in a later chapter, but here it is sufficient to record that, in the twentieth-century Western city, residential areas are notable for their social differences, which are in turn reflected in the structure and other characteristics of their populations. These population differences are produced by migration into and within cities, which reflects changes in the migrants' occupations, in their prosperity, in their social status, and in their housing requirements.

Many of the people who move into a typical growing city are young unmarried adults, who are attracted by the various "rooming house" districts in the urban area. The precise character of these migrants (and of the area in which they come to live) is influenced by the nature of employment in a particular city and the distance over which they have moved. For example, if the migration to the city has been over a long distance males are likely to predominate; if over a short distance females are more likely to be attracted by the city.

The effects of in-migration are most clearly seen where the migrants belong to an ethnic group different from that of the majority of a city's population. If the immigrants are separated from the rest of the population because of their race, language, religion or customs, they are likely to form themselves into distinct clusters, both for economic and social reasons. More often than not the members of these distinctive ethnic groups are employed in more poorly paid jobs, with the result that their homes are concentrated in the older residential areas, where deteriorating properties have declined in value and have been subdivided into smaller dwelling units. In addition, as immigrants of this kind are entering a strange social environment, they are attracted by areas in which their compatriots are already living. In such a location it may be easier for them to practise their religion and, if discrimination is practised, to find somewhere to live. Again, they may be drawn to particular districts by the simple attraction of having relatives and friends nearby, already established in an alien society.

Because such groups are socially different from the rest of the community, they often possess distinctive demographic characteristics. Because they are often poor and discriminated against, they tend to live at high densities in overcrowded conditions. If they have come from less advanced rural areas the fertility of communities like these is often higher than average and the number of children in the population greater. If proper allowance is made for the age structure of the immigrant population, they tend to have a higher than average death rate, presumably as a result of relative overcrowding and poverty. Yet the demographic and other distinctive features of these immigrant groups are likely to disappear in time unless similar people continue to move in, since in many cases the children of the immigrants tend to absorb much of the culture of the majority of the population.

One example of a group of this kind, which illustrates the various influences controlling its location, is provided by the Puerto Rican immigrants in New York. In general terms these people settled where low-cost housing was available. Running parallel to this economic motive was the social desire to live with members of their own family or with a neighbour from their homeland, who had crossed to the United States earlier. But the nature of their employment also influenced where they chose to live, close to express stops on the major subway routes. Most Puerto Ricans in New York are employed in the service trades, in hotels, restaurants and centrally located factories (particularly those connected with the clothing trade). This often means that they have to work irregular hours and require accessibility to central Manhattan. It is therefore essential for them to live close to a means of cheap transport, particularly one offering all-night services.

In United States' cities, however, distinctive residential areas formed by the immigration of negroes from elsewhere in the U.S.A. are much more important. These areas are commonly called "ghettos", although the term originally applied to Jewish areas in European cities; but the black ghettos differ from other distinctive ethnic areas in a number of ways. First, the numbers of people involved are much larger and the areas under almost exclusively black occupation are therefore much more extensive. Second, the inhabitants of the black ghettos are native-born Americans, with aspirations which in the last resort are similar to those of the rest of the population. Some ethnic groups which formerly occupied distinctive areas in American cities clustered together largely from choice, but the concentrations of negro population are often imposed by circumstances, rather than freely-chosen. Finally, the fact that the black population can be easily distinguished means that escape from ghetto conditions is much more difficult to achieve, even by people who have become more prosperous and who (if they were not so clearly "different") might well blend into the general population. As a result, natural increase of the black population, now an increasing source of additional black people in many American cities, tends to be contained in and around the existing ghetto areas.

These various features have meant that the outward expansion of black ghettos has assumed greater importance than is the case with other ethnic areas and this process of growth has attracted the attention of some geographers. R. L. Morrill, for example, has observed that there are identifiable zones around the ghetto: five or six blocks away nearly 100 per cent of house-purchasers are white, but in the so-called "break" zone over 60 per cent of purchasers may be black, although the existing black population in the area may be less than 5 per cent. Finally a zone is reached where all of the purchasers of property are black. Morrill has elaborated this observation to produce a statistical model which allows the simulation of the process of ghetto expansion. This is based on the underlying probability of the black population purchasing houses at varying distances from the ghetto edge, with suitable allowance being made for the amount of black immigration into the city, the rate of natural increase, the number of people which an individual block can absorb, and other housing characteristics. The ghetto areas, where nearly 100 per cent of the population is black, are not without internal variations. Because of their relatively large size and because their population cannot operate freely in the housing market of the whole city, some black areas in American cities have developed an internal social pattern of their own, independent of the rest of the city, with middle-income black population in different areas from the low-income population.

Intra-Urban Migration

The sorting-out of population by income groups is, of course, a normal and general feature of the Western city, and this process has demographic implications as well as social ones. Much of the increasing urban population of many Western countries is now produced by an excess of births over deaths in the cities themselves, rather than by immigration. Even so, areas with distinctive population characteristics still develop, since such areas are also produced by movements of population within the confines of individual cities (Fig. 15). The most important of these movements is the shift of population to new residential suburbs,* which are either built for private occupation or are provided for rent by local authorities.

Those who move into their own new houses are "selected" in two ways. First they are chosen by their ability to pay, a factor which broadly limits the purchase of new houses to middle-class people. These people in turn are sorted into houses of a range of sizes and located in areas of differing social desirability, their choice being controlled by the location of their places of work, by their family size, and by the amount that individual families can afford. In searching for a new home a house-purchaser is unlikely to have an equal amount of information about opportunities in every part of the city. Hence he is likely to move outwards in the same sector of the city in which he already lives and knows most about. Even among the well-off the demand to live in a new

* See Chapter 7.

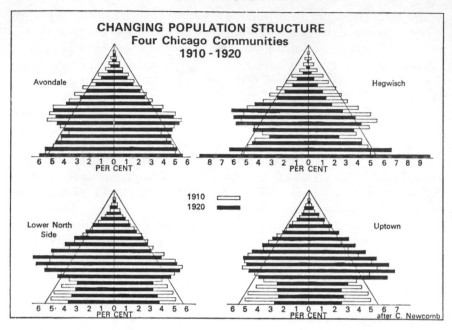

Fig. 15. Age and sex structure of four communities in Chicago, 1910 and 1920. (*Source*: Newcomb, *Bulletin of the Society for Social Research* (1938).)

The diagrams reproduced here are taken from an early study which stressed two features of demographic patterns within Chicago. One is the varying population structure in contrasting districts; the other is the manner in which these conditions may change over quite short periods.

These pyramids analyse the age and sex structure of four contrasting districts. Women are shown on the right-hand side of the diagrams; and the population is plotted in five-year age groups, youngest at the bottom.

Uptown was an apartment-hotel area of Chicago where absolute numbers increased by 113 per cent in the ten-year period. A notable feature is the increase in the proportion of women aged 21 to 44 and the decreasing proportion of children.

Lower North Side lost nearly 14 per cent of its population in the decade. In 1920 this was a rooming house district, which showed an increase in the proportion of adult men, but also recorded a decrease in the number of children in the population.

Hegwisch was a manufacturing district with a population increase of 40 per cent. The changing population of this area was largely due to natural increase, as the very large number of young children in its population indicates. There was also some movement of adult males into the area.

In *Avondale* population increased by nearly 42 per cent over the decade. In spite of this growth, it attracted substantially the same proportions of the age and sex groups it possessed in 1910, and its population structure was altered only slightly.

suburb does not become effective immediately. Young unmarried adults continue to live with their parents or in rooming-house areas until they marry and have children of their own. As a result, typical families moving into a new suburban estate consist of middle-class couples in their later twenties or early thirties, with one or two children. The quality of life on such an estate is largely conditioned by the resulting structure of population and society.

On the face of it, new houses built by local authorities present a more complex situation, since their residents may be drawn from families setting up home for the first time and also from those displaced by slum clearance. In fact, the people who move to public authority houses on the fringes of cities also pass through an economic filter, since these houses are less attractive for the poorest workers. Even with subsidized houses, living on the fringes of a city often involves a longer, more expensive journey to work and, in many cases, a higher rent than had previously been paid. As among the purchasers of middle-class homes, the desire to provide better conditions for their young families has been an important motive among many of those who have moved to suburban houses built by local authorities.

Because of this and because of the advantage given to them by local authorities in the allocation of houses, a high proportion of married couples with young families reside in these estates, which also contain an above average number of skilled workers. In Britain, where class differentials in fertility have been steadily reduced in the twentieth century, the resulting population structure is not greatly different from that on private enterprise housing estates, although the social contrasts still remain clear.

The demographic features of new housing estates of all kinds are emphasized by their lack of a past history, but as time passes the distinctive population pyramid of a newly built suburb takes on a more complex form. The original inhabitants become older and their children grow up and eventually leave home. Some houses change hands and a new generation of young adults joins the population. Thus the passage of time complicates the structure of population in the suburbs.

The selective relocation of population and the processes of time also affect the areas which population is leaving, as well as those to which it is moving. It may be that the people who move out of an area, because of a change in their status or income, are replaced by others who are similar to those already living there. Such a process would produce a relative static demographic situation; but in the long run the exact *status quo* is rarely maintained. Often a form of social "leap-frogging" takes place, with white-collar workers being eventually replaced by skilled manual workers who, in turn, may be succeeded by unskilled workers, each class having its own demographic and social characteristics.

In areas where continuing outward movement takes place without an equivalent in-migration, the population structure frequently becomes increasingly dominated by older people. Without the same family pressures to encourage a change in location, or possibly without the money to move, older residents tend to remain behind after their younger neighbours have moved out (Fig. 16). This selective process is not always a matter of age: areas of deteriorating property are often confirmed as zones of blight by the outward movement of law-abiding citizens, which frequently takes place in these circumstances. Where older working-class districts are being rebuilt the outward movement may be less selective, simply producing a lower density of population, since with modern standards of accommodation it is often impossible to rehouse everyone who lived in the area originally, even if high-rise flats are built.

Research on the population characteristics of the different internal regions of cities has received renewed interest in recent years as a result of the availability of census information by small enumeration districts and of the application of computers to the handling of data. As a result it has now become possible to analyse a considerable amount of detailed information concerning the population of cities, and also to quantify the various relationships that exist between such diverse features as social class, housing quality and demographic structure. What have become standardized procedures like component and factor analysis can be applied to grouping this information to form statistically meaningful regions.

The application of these more advanced statistical techniques to an immensely large body of data may well represent a step forward, since it may eventually allow general statements to be built up from detailed information for a wide range of cities. Yet, at the present stage of geographical work, it is doubtful if an important intellectual stride has in fact been taken. The data most commonly used is the socially incomplete collection made in census returns, and there is no assurance that the most important variables have been included in these analyses. Although it is now possible to map what has been called the "factorial ecology" of individual cities in much greater detail than was possible before, it is by no means certain that these inductive methods will produce better generalizations about the social patterns within cities;

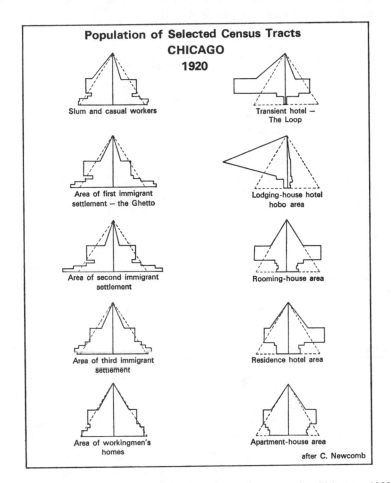

FIG. 16. Population structure of selected census tracts in Chicago, 1920. (*Source*: Newcomb, *Bulletin of the Society for Social Research* (1938).)

The diagrams (which are on the same basis as Fig. 15) attempt to illustrate types of age and sex structure found in Chicago in 1920. On the left are areas where the proportion of children was higher than in the United States as a whole, but where a variety of ecological situations existed. On the right are areas where adults were predominant, but represent a wide range of social conditions, ranging from the lodging house area (with its very large proportion of adult males) to the residential hotel area (an area characterized by prosperous widows, and families with few children but many servants).

nor is there any clear sign that they are revealing much about the processes which produce the patterns revealed.

Gradients of Population Density within Cities

The distribution of population within any city is complex in detail, but in most urban settlements it exhibits two notable features. One of these is the absence of residential population in the centres of modern Western cities;* the other is the falling population density found on a traverse from the inner parts of cities to their peripheries. This decline in density follows a regular pattern: Colin Clark has shown that in a wide range of cities, with a variety of locations and at different times in the past, population density decreases at a constant rate with increasing distance from the city centre. In other words, if density and linear distance from the centre are plotted on a graph a negative exponential curve is produced (Fig. 17).†

Two important assumptions are involved in this generalization. For one thing, the absence of residential population in the centre is disregarded and an assumed central density is calculated, based on the density gradient in the outer residential areas. This assumption is useful in allowing simpler statistical analysis of the varying density gradients found in different cities; but it is sometimes overlooked that the central density is merely a convention.

A second assumption is implied by the manner in which the statistics are processed for individual cities. Normally the densities used are the averages for a number of census areas, grouped in concentric rings at successive distances from the city centre. Such a calculation assumes that those parts of a city which are the same distance from the centre also possess a similar morphology. There is evidence that the form of cities is more complex than this, particularly in the larger, more complex, metropolitan centres. Hence there is a danger that the average densities may hide important differences.

Recent work has confirmed the validity of Clark's original generalization and extended its application. It has been shown, for example, that accessibility to the city centre is probably more important than simple linear distance in controlling the densities of population found. It has been suggested that, the larger the city, the higher will be the central

---

* See Chapter 6.

† Expressed in mathematical terms $P_d = P_0 e^{-md}$ (where P_d is the density at distance d from the city centre, P_0 is the extrapolated central density, m is the density gradient, and e is the base of the natural logarithms).

densities (although the fact that this is an assumed density should be borne in mind here). Other work has traced the manner in which the density gradient has become less steep in modern cities. The collection of further information has also led to suggestions that the precise form of the density gradient is more precisely expressed by a formula which relates density to the square of the distance from the city centre.* Further elaboration has come from the work of B. Newling,† in which he attempts to find a mathematical expression which represents the development of the density "crater" around the city centre with the passage of time, although perhaps in the process he complicates the original simple description unnecessarily, without producing a commensurate gain in the precision with which his equation fits reality. Attempts have also been made to provide a theoretical explanation for the existence of the density gradient.

One approach attempts to explain the gradient in purely economic terms. Putting it very simply, it is argued that the most desirable, and hence most expensive, sites for all urban land uses lie close to the city

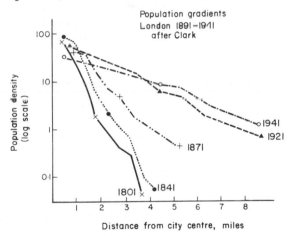

Fig. 17. London: population density and distance from city centre, 1801–1941. (*Source*: Clark, *Journal of Royal Statistical Society*, **A114** (1951), 490.)

centre, where maximum accessibility is provided by converging transport routes. The further a site is from the city centre, the greater are the transport costs involved in its use; but because of reduced competition the cost of such sites is lower. These lower land values encourage lower intensity of use away from the centre, particularly as less intensive land uses cannot compete effectively for the more expensive, inner sites. This

* The equation then becomes $P_d = P_0 e^{-md^2}$.

† B. E. Newling, The spatial variation of urban population densities, *Geographical Review* **59** (1969), 242–52.

argument applies to the use of land for residence as well as for other purposes; and lower intensities of residential land use produce lower densities of population towards the peripheries of cities.

It is also suggested that in Western cities this situation is reinforced by the typical location of different social groups within a city. The poor find transport costs a more important part of their budget than do the rich, and they tend to live closer to the centre where they have more immediate accessibility to their jobs. As a result they can only afford to consume relatively small amounts of this more expensive land for their homes, and thus live at high densities. The rich, on the other hand, can afford the time, cost and inflexibility of a longer daily journey from the periphery to the centre. On the outskirts of a city land is cheaper, but individually the rich consume more of it for their larger and more widely spaced houses. Hence this factor, too, tends to produce a falling density gradient from the inner to the outer residential areas.

But an explanation of this kind can at best be only a partial one, since it neglects at least two important aspects of urban geography. One is the historical process of urban development: a city is not created instantaneously to meet the current demands of economy and society, but includes contributions from past periods in its fabric. These contributions from the past reflect former means of transport and earlier ideas of the densities appropriate for residential building. Thus even without the modern patterns of land values and social grouping within a city, there would be a tendency for lower densities in the newer than in the older residential areas.

A second feature which tends to be overlooked in these explanations is that accessibility in the modern city can no longer be measured simply in terms of distance from the centre. Particularly around the fringes of large cities, suburban manufacturing and retailing have greatly increased, producing urban settlements which are often multi-centred in form. This is one factor producing more gradual density gradients by increasing the attraction of the suburbs and at the same time lowering that of the centre. Nor can accessibility be measured simply by ease of access to jobs and shops. Part of the attraction of modern low density suburbs is connected with their access to open space—a factor which complicates the detailed pattern of land values in these areas.

Most work on the gradient of population density has been concerned with the cities of Europe, North America and Australia, but recently Berry, Simmons and Tennant have made an interesting attempt to compare the density gradients found in Western and non-Western cities. Their view is that, while both types of city show a negative exponential relationship between density and distance from the city centre, the manner in which their gradients have developed over the last century has been different (Fig. 18). In Western cities the density gradient began to decrease in the last quarter of the nineteenth century and this trend has been greatly accelerated in the twentieth century. Although central densities may have increased at first, they later decreased, and the extent of low density outer suburbs has greatly expanded. In non-Western cities, on the other hand, the central density continued to rise through time, and the density gradient has remained relatively constant. Not only has the distribution of population remained relatively compact, but central densities have actually increased.

The explanation of this difference has been sought in two features of non-Western cities. One is their less flexible system of transport, which has encouraged the maintenance of more compact cities. The other is the different organization of their society, in which the richer people still wish to live close to the centre, rather than on the periphery. As a result there is a greater demand for central sites for residential purposes as non-Western cities grow in size, and greater central densities of population result. The poorer and less mobile social groups are pushed out to the periphery, but they cannot afford suburban life on the Western

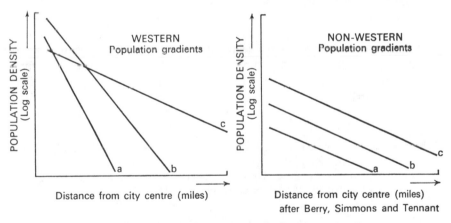

FIG. 18. Comparative diagrams of density–distance relationships in "Western" and "non-Western" cities. (*Source*: Berry, Simmons and Tennant, *Geographical Review* **53** (1963), 403.)

pattern and live at relatively higher densities. As a result it has been suggested that there has been little change in the population gradient of these cities with the passage of time, since both suburban and central densities have increased as the cities have expanded.

This contrast is interesting, but it is open to dispute whether it is fully justified. For example, some confusion comes from the use of the terms "Western" and "non-Western"—an Indian city like Calcutta has much in common with many Western cities in terms of its size and socio-economic organization, but it has been used as an example of a non-Western city. Indeed, where pre-European cities in Asia have grown greatly in size, their morphology usually contains elements of both Western and indigenous cultures.* In such a situation average densities, calculated at fixed distances from the city centre, are particularly likely to hide more than they reveal. There is also some evidence that the proposed "Western" pattern of changing gradients is not exclusively Western, and that the "non-Western" pattern is not exclusively non-Western.† At the moment all that can be said conclusively is that the nature of local society and its economic processes affect the internal distribution of population within cities.

Indeed, the general conclusion of this chapter must be that the local history of population and the resulting distribution of class, ethnic and religious groups produce variations in the demographic characteristics of different parts of a city. These variations are not isolated from other social and economic phenomena, but are merely indications of a variety of ecological situations. In other words, demographic characteristics are only one element in forming these distinctive areas and are closely connected with a whole series of other features, such as the incidence of delinquency, differing levels of prosperity and the size and nature of dwellings. It is for this reason that the various internal regions of a city, each with their own distinctive townscapes, possess equally distinctive population structures.

Selected Reading

A large number of research articles relevant to this chapter are collected in

R. K. HATT and A. J. REISS Jr. (eds.), *Cities and Society: the Revised Reader in Urban Sociology* (2nd edition, New York, 1957). See especially section 5, The demographic structure and vital processes, pp. 311–92.

Rural–urban contrasts are summarized in

P. H. MANN, *An Approach to Urban Sociology* (London, 1965), chapters 2 and 3.

The relation between city function and demographic characteristics is explored for the United States in

H. J. NELSON, Some characteristics of the population of cities in similar service classifications, *Economic Geography* **33** (1957), 95–108.

A study of a particular city, which examines (among other topics) internal population variations, is

E. JONES, *A Social Geography of Belfast* (London, 1960).

---

* See below, pp. 178–80.

† See, for example, B. E. Newling, Urban population densities and intra-urban growth, *Geographical Review* **54** (1964), 440–2.

The location of an immigrant group in New York is analysed in

> R. T. NOVAK, Distribution of Puerto Ricans on Manhattan Island, *Geographical Review* **46** (1956), 182–6.

An important study which examines the process of ghetto expansion in U.S. cities is

> R. L. MORRILL, The negro ghetto: alternatives and consequences, *Geographical Review* **55** (1965), 221–38.

The role of search behaviour in shaping the pattern of ghetto expansion is investigated in

> H. M. ROSE, The development of an urban subsystem: the case of the negro ghetto, *Annals of the Association of American Geographers* **60** (1970), 1–17.

More general considerations in the process of population moves within urban areas are examined in

> J. W. SIMMONS, Changing residence in the city: a review of intra-urban mobility, *Geographical Review* **58** (1968), 622–51.

A very useful summary dealing with a particular case is

> H. M. ROSE, *Social Processes in the City: Race and Residential Choice* (Association of American Geographers, Resource Paper no. 6, 1969).

Gradients of population density within cities are examined in

> C. CLARK, Urban population densities, *Journal of the Royal Statistical Society*, series A, **114** (1951), 490–6.

A comparison between "Western" and "non-Western" population gradients is made in

> B. L. J. BERRY *et al.*, Urban population densities: structure and change, *Geographical Review* **53** (1963), 389–405.

The form of the gradient is given an economic rationale in

> W. ALONSO, A theory of the urban land market, *Papers and Proceedings, Regional Science Association* **6** (1960), 149–58.

> H. H. WINSBOROUGH, City growth and city structure, *Journal of Regional Sciences* **4** (1962), 35–49.

> R. F. MUTH, The spatial structure of the housing market, *Papers and Proceedings, Regional Science Association* **7** (1962), 207–20.

Factorial ecology is discussed and a particular example is examined in detail in

> R. A. MURDIE, *Factorial Ecology of Metropolitan Toronto, 1951–1961: An Essay on the Social Geography of the City* (University of Chicago, Dept. of Geography Research Paper no. 116, Chicago, 1969).

See also the various articles in "Comparative Factorial Ecology", *Economic Geography* **47**, no. 2 (Supplement), June 1971.

CHAPTER 4

OCCUPATIONAL CHARACTERISTICS OF URBAN POPULATIONS

Towns and cities owe their existence to the presence of certain social and economic activities which require the concentration of people, buildings and machines within relatively small areas. These activities, and the types of employment associated with them, can be described as being distinctively "urban"; and hence an important characteristic of urban populations is provided by the occupations which they follow.

Although pre-industrial cities undertook a considerable number of functions, they were based on a simple handicraft economy and were served by a relatively unelaborate system of communications. As a result, although their inhabitants were employed in a wide range of occupations, the structure of employment in these cities was much simpler than in the modern world, both in terms of size of labour force and division of labour.

With the recent change from a rural to a predominantly urban mode of living in the industrialized countries of the world, a many-layered structure of employment has developed in cities. This greater complexity is associated with the more sophisticated division of labour found in modern industry (not only in the processes of manufacture but also in distribution), the stronger links between urban areas and their surroundings, and the greater demands made upon urban services in an age of more general affluence.

Thus the occupational structure of most cities exhibits vestiges of the old handicraft industries; and to these must be added the labour force engaged in modern manufacturing industry. A further layer is provided by those workers who render services to customers living outside the urban area; and, in addition, a proportion of those in the service occupations are concerned with catering for the population of the city itself. Finally there is usually an adventitious population of varying size which does not make its living in the city but merely resides there.

The Structure of Urban Occupations

Although large-scale manufacturing is fundamental to modern urban growth, this occupation may not necessarily be found in particular cities. Activities connected with the exchange of goods and services, however, lie at the basis of all towns, ancient and modern. This trading function is reflected in the characteristic location of urban settlements on transport routes, on the boundaries between major natural regions, and at the centres of their own local spheres of influence.* For trade to take place facilities must exist in a town or city to allow the buying and selling of goods, and means of transport must be available to allow their import and export. In turn, the occupations associated with trade support a range of ancillary activities. For example, the means of transport require to be serviced if they are to function efficiently, and loading and unloading have to be undertaken. Similarly, the sorting and storing of goods are inseparable from the processes of buying and selling, as are occupations connected with finance and insurance.

As production has become more efficient because of mechanization, it has been necessary to expand the market for manufactured and other goods in order to absorb production. At the same time production has also become more specialized and, therefore, both raw materials and manufactured goods have needed to be transported over longer distances and in greater quantities than ever before. As a result, institutions connected with transport and trade have expanded most rapidly in those strategic locations which command a large market and provide links in the interchange of goods over long distances. Specialization in production, the development of trade, and urban growth are all closely interrelated; and the total number of urban dwellers engaged in trade and transport has grown as efficient distribution has become vitally important for industrial prosperity. This trend is particularly notable in large cities, which are often major ports.

In ancient cities manufacturing was less important than trade, but after the technological changes associated with the industrial revolution, the new economics of large-scale production encouraged the development of larger units of production and larger labour forces. As a result, manufacturing industry became a most important cause of urban growth in Europe and North America and the single most important occupation of urban dwellers in these areas. At the same time the division of labour in many manufacturing processes was taken further, with the result that certain types of occupations, particularly those connected in various

* See Chapter 5.

ways with the production of specialized goods, tended to group together in particular urban settlements.

The development of specialist cities depended on the improvement of transport by road, rail and sea. With cheaper, faster and more reliable methods of shifting freight and with the progressive removal of trade barriers, the point of extraction of raw materials, the point of fabrication and the point of final consumption for many products could be widely separated. As a result many kinds of manufacturing were undertaken at their most economical locations. Paradoxically enough, this greater freedom of location often increased the advantages of concentration, since the external economies provided by specialist groups of industrial towns frequently proved a dominant factor in industrial location. Industrial cities, once established, tended to attract more industry, frequently of the same or of a closely linked type.

In addition to occupations connected with trade and manufacturing, most urban settlements have also attracted a range of ancillary urban activities. Sometimes these have provided the main growing points in the economies of particular urban centres, but much more often they have been attracted by the presence of businesses already there. Possibly the most important of these ancillary occupations are those connected with finance. Without the presence of general banking facilities and the provision of credit, the development of modern trade and manufacturing industry would be virtually impossible. Similarly, the presence of institutions which facilitate investment have become particularly important with the growth of public companies and the development of complex financial links between related firms.

In addition to those occupations directly concerned with finance, there are other ancillary business activities, closely connected with manufacturing and trade, which are carried out by independent concerns. Some of these enterprises are relatively small, like lawyers, business consultants, advertising agents and accountants, whose services are necessary to allow modern industry to function smoothly. Others form much larger units, as for instance insurance companies, whose risk-bearing function is essential for the security of many other enterprises, and also the headquarters of national and international companies, which require the accessibility best found in metropolitan centres.

A third group of workers in ancillary occupations provide personal services. Some of these services are used by residents living within the limits of a city and some are also used by people from outside the built-up area. Although for the purpose of studying the urban economic base it would be useful to be able to distinguish between these two groups of customers, in practice this is almost impossible, since the same employees serve them both, often without making any distinction between the two. Doctors, personal servants, teachers and workers in restaurants and laundries all provide examples of this type of occupation.

A final group of activities is concerned with providing more general services, which may well be important to industrialists as well as individual urban residents. For example, workers employed by power stations and by municipal transport and water companies provide services without which modern urban life would be impossible. Those workers providing fire protection, safeguarding public health and manning police forces fall into a similar class. Employees in public administration also provide general services to the community at large, although they are numerically most important in the capital city and in larger regional centres.

The Basic/Non-basic Concept

Some of the efforts of the inhabitants of a town or city are concerned with serving people living outside it, thus bringing wealth into the community. The rest of their efforts are aimed at serving the population of the settlement itself. As a result a case has been made for dividing the economic activities of urban communities into two formal categories. Some authorities have called these two sectors of the urban economy "primary" and "secondary", others have used the terms "city-building" and "service", but these terms are difficult to use, as they can easily be confused with the economist's division of employment into primary, secondary and tertiary types. As a result the usual terms now used are "basic" and "non-basic".

The obvious basic elements in a city's economy include those people manufacturing for an external market, that is, one lying outside the limits of the settlement. In this same sector are included those who provide services rather than manufactured goods for customers living outside the town. The non-basic sector is concerned with meeting the needs of a city's own inhabitants, and thus includes certain kinds of manufacturing for the local market, as well as such services as local transport and retailing. Workers in the non-basic sector must in no sense be seen as unnecessary, since without them an urban settlement would cease to function. The non-basic sector is so termed merely because it depends on money brought into the community by the basic sector of the economy.

Considerable attention has been given to this aspect of the urban economy, largely stimulated by two motives, one academic and the other practical. The academic interest has been to illuminate more

clearly the way in which the population of an urban settlement is supported. The basic population has been seen as maintaining the non-basic
population, which in turn requires a further layer of non-basic population to serve it. If this is so, it would be interesting to separate out the
basic workers in a city, since their presence provides the *raison d'être* of
the urban settlement and supports a varying number of non-basic
workers. It is also argued that if the normal ratio between basic and
non-basic workers can be established for different types and sizes of
city, it should lead to a better understanding of the size of a city's total
population.

Practical interest follows from this, since the future space requirements
of a city will be connected with the nature of its economic base. It has
been suggested that, if the basic and non-basic ratio of a particular city
is known and if some reasonable prediction can be made of the future
expansion of the basic segment of its economy, then it should be possible
to calculate the future total population, thus allowing various planning
decisions to be made in the light of this forecast. To give a very simple
example: if there are 1000 basic workers in a city to 2000 non-basic
workers, and if it is known that a firm which will employ 200 more basic
workers is to be located there, then an assumption can be made that the
non-basic sector will also expand by 400 workers, giving a total population increase of 600 (plus their dependents). But while the basic/non-
basic concept, as this approach to the structure of urban occupations
has been called, may form an acceptable basis for a rough calculation,
there are considerable practical and theoretical difficulties associated
with it, both as a statement of the nature of the urban economy and as a
tool for prediction.

One obvious practical difficulty is that of discovering the basic/non-
basic ratio in a particular city, since the division between these two
sectors runs across the boundaries of formal occupational groups.
Various methods have been devised to solve this problem by the manipulation of published statistics, the most recent and one of the most
interesting of these being the "Minimum Requirements Method" devised by E. Ullman and M. Dacey.

Their method was to classify the cities of the United States into size
groups and then to examine the percentage of the total labour force
which was employed in each of the fourteen occupational categories
listed in the United States census. The lowest percentage recorded by
any city within each group for these various occupations was assumed to
be the minimum necessary to enable cities of that order of size to
function (Fig. 19). These minimum requirements were equated with
the non-basic population; and in an individual city the number of

workers over the minimum necessary to maintain its viability was taken to represent its basic population.

Another approach to the solution of this problem is to gather information by special field-work in individual cities. One method of this type is to make a sample survey of the various enterprises in an urban area,

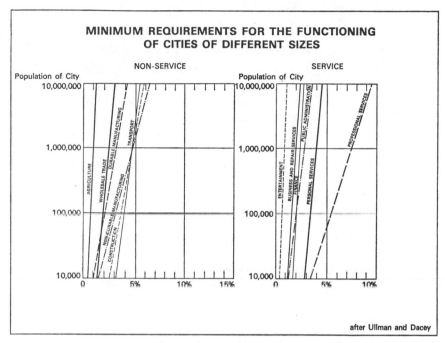

Fig. 19. United States cities: the minimum requirements for the functioning of urban settlements of different sizes. (*Source*: Ullman and Dacey, in *I.G.U. Symposium in Urban Geography* (1962), p. 129.)

The *x*-axis of these graphs shows the percentage of the total working population which is employed in certain occupations. The figures plotted represent the minimum percentages in these different occupational types, found in various size-groups of United States cities. These proportions are shown to vary with the size of the city; and it is assumed that, taken together, they represent the minimum number of workers of different types which are necessary to allow a city of a particular size to function.

designed to discover the size of their labour force and the percentage of their total sales made in the local urban market. The labour force in the city is then divided into basic and non-basic sectors, in relation to the proportion of sales made locally. An alternative method is to study the finances of a city, rather than its workers, although information of this kind is very difficult to obtain. One early example of this method is the survey of Oskaloosa in Iowa—a town with a mere 10,000 inhabitants—carried out by *Fortune* Magazine.* In this study the sources of income of the community were established by means of numerous interviews and questionnaires. The total income of the town was set alongside the amount derived from non-local sources, to allow a basic/non-basic ratio to be established.

Theoretical Objections to the Basic/Non-basic Concept

In the last resort, however, great refinement in method is of little point, since there are serious theoretical difficulties which undermine the effective use of the basic/non-basic concept. To start with, the limits given to a particular settlement are of great importance in distinguishing basic from non-basic activities; but the larger the size of

TABLE 1. THE BASIC/NON-BASIC RATIO OF CERTAIN UNITED STATES CITIES
(AFTER J. ALEXANDER)

City	Total population	Basic/Non-basic ratio
New York	12,500,000	100 : 215
Detroit	2,900,000	100 : 117
Cincinnati	907,000	100 : 170
Brockton	119,000	100 : 82
Albuquerque	116,000	100 : 103
Madison	110,000	100 : 82
Oshkosh	42,000	100 : 60

Source: J. Alexander, *Econ. Geog.* **30** (1954), 259.

the city, the more likely it is that there will be a greater amount of non-basic activity. This is because the larger a city, the more liable it is to be economically diversified, and more business will be done between firms and individuals within the city's limits. Table 1 illustrates some of the basic/non-basic ratios found in United States cities: the major conclusion which appears to emerge is that the ratio bears a fairly direct relationship to the size of city being studied.

In modern urban areas the problem of limits is particularly difficult, since it is rare for the built-up area to coincide with a city's legal boundaries. This technical difficulty is even more serious if a city forms part of a cluster of urban settlements. Today, with modern communications and the free exchange of goods and services, an urban area may be

* Oskaloosa versus the United States, *Fortune*, April 1938, pp. 55 ff.

physically separate from its neighbours, but linked by such close economic and social ties that they all form part of the same system of urban production. In such circumstances it would be inappropriate to take the limits of a single city in calculating the basic/non-basic ratio. A dormitory settlement, perhaps with very little local basic employment, may be a very prosperous town with a high rate of growth. A specialized industrial town will have a very large number of basic workers, since most of its products are likely to be sold outside its own limits, but this does not necessarily reveal anything significant about its economic well-being.

A second theoretical difficulty is associated with the separation of basic and non-basic workers. Many individual workers undertake both activities as part of their daily round and, even with careful field-work, the distinction is often artificial. For that matter, many workers, who can be unequivocally classified as non-basic, make a very important contribution to basic output. The employees in a local water undertaking or power station are often providing their services exclusively for the local urban market, but their efforts also provide essential raw materials for basic industrial production. To all intents and purposes these workers take part in the process of basic production.

Even if the basic/non-basic ratio is assessed in terms of sales made, rather than by the number of workers in each sector, again only a crude indication is given of the economic health of a town or city. The amount of wealth brought into an urban centre cannot be calculated merely in terms of the value of goods sold to the outside world, since the cost of the materials used in production must also be allowed for. The contribution of a factory, which is concerned with assembling high-value components produced elsewhere, cannot be assessed from the total selling price of its products.

As the simple division of urban occupations into two segments is conceptually weak, it is not surprising that the basic/non-basic ratio provides only a blunt tool for predicting future developments. The economy of an urban settlement does not usually depend on one single industry, and the basic/non-basic concept gives no help at all in distinguishing which of a number of individual firms are most vulnerable to outside competition and which are most likely to expand in the future. Even a simple calculation of the probable change in the total population of a city to be expected from an increase in its basic employment is not completely valid, since it does not follow that the basic/non-basic ratio will remain the same in an enlarged settlement. Indeed, there is evidence that the ratio is unstable during a period of urban expansion. For example, a growth in the basic population of a city might well be catered for by an expansion in the productivity of non-basic workers, rather than in their number. Over a period of time, too, non-basic activities may expand sufficiently to acquire "basic" characteristics: a local bakery may increasingly sell its products to a non-local market, or an enterprising shop may acquire a larger number of out-of-town customers. As a result, the use of the basic/non-basic ratio to calculate future population totals is very suspect, except perhaps in the simplest cases, where intuitive methods would work just as well.

An alternative approach is clearly necessary, and one is now being provided by the technique of studying the flow of goods, money and services in an economy which was devised by W. W. Leontief and is known as input–output analysis. In simple terms this is a method of tabulating economic facts so that the exchange of goods and services among all the various parts of an economy can be comprehended. This mode of analysis should allow the ramifications of a change in one particular activity to be analysed; but a major difficulty comes with the assembly and processing of the necessary data and with the development of appropriate methods of using this analysis to predict future trends, although modern high-speed computers have partly solved this technical problem.

So far, input–output analysis has usually been applied to national or, at least, regional economies; but there is no theoretical reason why it should not be applied to individual cities. Indeed, a number of attempts have been made to do this, but it is fair to say that this approach is still at the experimental stage. The greatest difficulties at this scale lie in defining an appropriate area for study and in acquiring accurate, detailed information about the workings of a particular urban economy. Work is also still continuing on the development of suitable mathematical "models" of the urban economy which will allow the relative importance of various activities and processes to be built into statistical predictions of future trends. One important practical application of this approach should be a means of forecasting the impact of a particular alteration in the economic base on the general pattern of economic activity in a city.

Occupations and the Classification of Cities

Although most urban areas have at least a few workers in a wide range of occupations, the balance between different activities varies greatly from city to city. As a result, urban occupations have often been used for the classification of towns and cities into different functional types. The functional classification of cities has a long history—pioneer work in this field was undertaken as long ago as 1841—but the purposes for which various classifications have been designed has not always been made clear by their authors. Looking over the various attempts that have been made, certain reasons for urban classification emerge. One important purpose has been to make more comprehensible the mass of occupational statistics now available for many cities. A second reason has been to allow a better understanding of the location of cities, since this can be properly analysed only in relation to the function which a particular city offers. Finally, urban classifications have been used to examine the relationship between a city's dominant function and other features of its geography (like, for instance, its population structure).

Early approaches to functional classification often merely consisted of the subjective application of descriptive labels. Urban settlements were categorized as manufacturing cities, commercial centres, resorts, university towns and so on, without any real analysis of their occupational structure. Apart from its very arbitrary nature, such a method does not allow for the fact that most towns have many functions, and that the most obvious function is not necessarily the most important. In reality the shops of a mining town may make it a more important centre of retail trade than of extractive industry, or manufacturing may be more important than education in a so-called university town.

The availability of detailed statistics in many countries has encouraged the development of quantitative methods, in which common statistical standards are applied to groups of cities. Many of these statistical classifications are simple and rapid to apply, one of the earliest and most influential being that devised by C. D. Harris in 1943 and applied to the U.S. census of 1930. Harris attempted to distinguish the most important single function in individual cities, judging this by the proportion of the population employed in certain occupations, and thus giving specific quantitative meanings to the functional labels he devised. The most important function could not simply be taken as that which employed the highest proportion of the population: for example, if a certain percentage of the employed population in wholesaling allowed one city to be called a "wholesaling centre" the same proportion employed in manufacturing in another city would not be sufficient to allow it to be described as "manufacturing centre".

To overcome this difficulty, Harris examined the occupational structure of a number of cities which, in his view, fell into well-defined types. He then used these results as a basis for classifying other cities. For instance, he reckoned that a settlement could be classified as a "manufacturing centre" if at least 60 per cent of its total employment in manufacturing, retailing and wholesaling was in manufacturing. On the other hand, a "retail centre" had to have at least 50 per cent of its employed population in retailing; and in a "wholesaling centre" only 20 per cent needed to be employed in wholesaling. Using these same percentages Harris also recognized "diversified cities", in which employment in manufacturing was less than 60 per cent of the total, that in retailing less than 50 per cent, and that in wholesaling less than 20 per cent. Rather similar methods were used to recognize "transport cities", "mining cities" and "university cities". "Resort and retirement centres" were distinguished in the first place by the low percentage of their populations in any kind of employment; and their true function was confirmed by a search of the geographical literature.

As one end-product of this work, Harris attempted a general analysis of the location of the cities of the U.S.A. Very briefly, those cities which emerged as "manufacturing centres" were often located in a belt of cities concentrated in the north-east of the United States and along the Piedmont Belt. His "retail centres" were mostly smaller cities, lying outside the manufacturing belt and located at the centres of relatively small regions. "Wholesale centres" were either small cities engaged in the collection of agricultural products, or were larger cities like Denver and Salt Lake City, whose function was distribution. These bigger wholesaling cities were often the regional centres of larger areas (Fig. 20).

Certain objections can be raised against this method of classification. First, the classification does not permit the recognition of every possible type of urban settlement, largely because it depends on the form in which employment statistics were published in the United States. For example, "regional centres" were split among wholesaling, diversified and manufacturing cities, although there were forty-one such cities in the United States in the 1930's. Even allowing for the nature of the statistics, it can be argued that the labels attached to many urban settlements often hid more about their occupational structure than they revealed. For example, 80 per cent of the largest cities in the United States proved to be "diversified" cities, and indeed this diversification must have been an important factor in explaining their large size. But these large cities were the most important manufacturing, wholesaling and retailing centres in the nation, and they were also the most important educational and transportational centres. Hence the idea of attaching a simple descriptive label is particularly invalid in the case of these large complex cities.

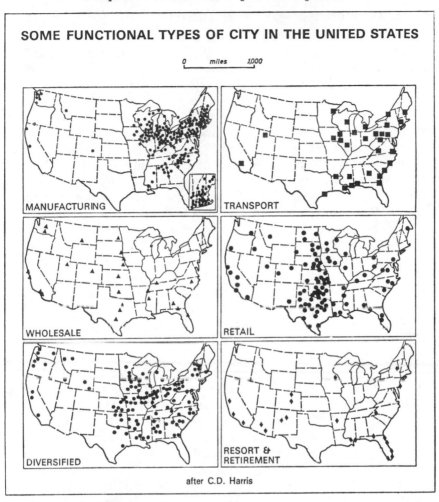

SOME FUNCTIONAL TYPES OF CITY IN THE UNITED STATES

0   miles   1,000

MANUFACTURING

TRANSPORT

WHOLESALE

RETAIL

DIVERSIFIED

RESORT &
RETIREMENT

after C.D. Harris

FIG. 20. United States cities: the distribution of some different functional
types. (*Source*: Harris, *Geographical Review* **33** (1943), 92.)

Harris's classification shed some light on the general location of cities
within the U.S.A. For example, cities classified as "manufacturing centres"
concentrated in the north-east and in the Piedmont belt; his "retail centres"
lay outside the manufacturing belt and were often at the centre of small
regions; and "wholesaling centres" were either small cities engaged in the
collection of agricultural products or were larger centres whose function
was distribution.

Recent Developments in Urban Classification

Later classifications have attempted to avoid some of these difficulties, in particular the arbitrary method of arriving at critical values. One example of such an attempt is given by L. L. Pownall's analysis of the function of New Zealand towns. In making this classification the average occupational structure found in towns of different sizes was calculated; and specialization in a particular function was indicated by the percentage deviation of an individual town from the average.

Such a method recognized that an important factor in classifying the function of an urban centre was the employment of an abnormal percentage of its population in a single occupational group, although the choice of the precise deviation from the average considered to be significant remained a matter for subjective judgement. It was also a useful idea to allow for the size of the settlement in assessing the occupational structure of various towns; but the fact that there are very few towns in certain of the groups makes their average structure of employment a less secure point of departure. The final result of this study, too, was handicapped by the considerable uniformity exhibited by these towns, leading to the somewhat unsatisfactory conclusion that New Zealand towns are predominantly multi-functional.

Later work, notably by H. J. Nelson in the United States and W. Steigenga in the Netherlands, has developed the use of the arithmetic mean as a basis for classification. For example, Nelson grouped the occupations of the urban population of the United States into nine major categories and calculated the average percentage in each category, using the 1950 census as the basis for his work. In addition he calculated the standard deviation shown by the statistics for each of these occupational groups. A settlement was recognized as specialized in a particular function if it contained the average percentage of people in that occupational group, plus one measure of standard deviation. As a result Nelson was able to apply an objective standard which identified a statistically significant deviation from the average.

The most important use made of this system was to distinguish those American cities which were outstanding for particular functions, and then to examine the extent to which other features of their population were related to this occupational specialization.* For this purpose the method was satisfactory, but the general principle of using average conditions as a basis for urban classifications is open to some criticism. The difficulty is that, if an average or some other critical limit is chosen, there is a danger of splitting up groups of similar towns which happen to fall on either side of the particular value chosen.

* See Chapter 3, pp. 49–50.

R. H. T. Smith has made this point convincingly with reference to a hypothetical graph, on which two occupational characteristics useful in urban classifications have been plotted. On this graph it is assumed that a series of cities are to be classified by the percentages of their populations employed in manufacturing and commerce (Fig. 21, a). If average conditions are to be the basis of a functional classification, a simple method would be to group these cities into four types:

    I. Above average in manufacturing and commerce.
   II. Above average in manufacturing, below average in commerce.
  III. Below average in manufacturing and commerce.
  IV. Below average in manufacturing, above average in commerce.

Although this grouping is logically attractive, it misses the point that in this hypothetical example the settlements fall naturally into four distinct

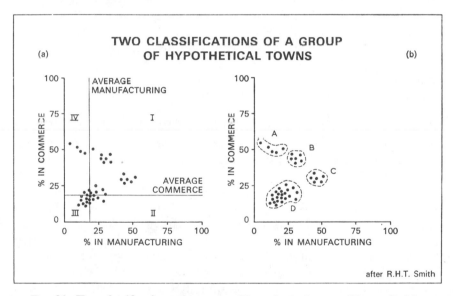

Fig. 21. Two classifications of a group of hypothetical towns. (*Source*: Smith, *Annals of The Association of American Geographers* **55** (1965), 543.)

groups, in each of which the individual settlements are very similar to one another (Fig. 21, b). This important grouping is hidden by a system of classification based on deviation from the average.

As a result, different methods are preferable if the aim of classification is to group together urban centres with the greatest functional similarity, rather than to distinguish a dominant function. A sophisticated approach to this problem is exemplified by a recent study of the demographic and socio-economic features of British towns carried out by C. A. Moser and Wolf Scott. Fifty-seven different items of relevant statistical information were assembled for each of 157 towns and cities in England and Wales with a population of over 50,000. To this data the technique of "component analysis" was applied, by which the fifty-seven variables were simplified into four components, which tended to vary independently of one another.

Using these four components, urban areas in England and Wales were grouped statistically, so that the settlements within each group were more similar to each other than to those in any other group. In other words, there was more difference between groups than between the members of any single group. It was possible to group 155 out of the 157 towns and cities. These 155 centres fell into three main clusters, which could be subdivided to give fourteen groups in all. This classification was based on demographic and socio-economic criteria, but it was found that functional labels could be attached to the groupings produced by these statistical processes. Some, for example, would be characterized as "newer industrial suburbs", others as "large ports", others as "seaside resorts" and so on. But the aim of this classification was not to arrive at simple functional types of this kind: if so, a mountain of effort would have brought forth only a mouse of a conclusion. The real purpose of this exercise, and its interest here, was to render comprehensible a vast body of statistical material by means of statistically valid procedures.

A later application of a similar method, but designed expressly to produce a geographical analysis of cities, is found in Chauncy Harris's study of cities in the U.S.S.R. As part of this work 30 characteristics derived from the Soviet 1959 census were examined for the 1247 cities which then had a population of more than 10,000 people. This information was then subjected to principal components analysis, which showed that a high proportion of the variation between cities could be accounted for by three components, apparently associated with distinctive geographical influences. One was a "size" component, most closely connected with population totals; a second was "density", most closely associated with the urban population potential* of each city within its major economic region; and a third was to do with "growth", being

---

* Population potential is calculated by the formula $P = \sum \dfrac{p}{d}$ where P is the population potential of a point, p is the population of each unit within the area for which the potential is being calculated, and d is the distance of each unit from the point.

most directly associated with population increase between 1926 and 1959. The "size" component made its influence felt by the manner in which the largest cities had diversified functions, being important manufacturing and administrative centres as well as occupying critical locations in the communications network. The "density" component indicated those cities that tended to cluster at localized sources of raw materials or in industrial districts with relatively long histories. Finally the "growth" component tended to pick out those cities of the eastern U.S.S.R. whose expansion has been relatively recent and which indicate the colonization of the east by urban life.

Another problem in classifying cities by their occupations has been that of distinguishing those activities which are found in all cities, regardless of their dominant function, from those which are concentrated in specialized settlements. One approach to this problem has been to classify cities by the occupations of their "basic" workers, on the grounds that this segment of its economy stresses the relations between a city and the outside world. For example, J. W. Maxwell has classified Canadian cities in this way, using the minimum requirements method to filter out the basic workers from the total labour force. If the object of classification is to shed more light on the location of settlements there is some justification in this method, particularly in the Canadian situation. Here, except possibly around Toronto, there is no integrated urban system of the kind found in the Manufacturing Belt of the United States or in Lowland Britain, so that the general difficulties associated with the basic/non-basic concept do not loom too large.

J. W. Webb also recognized this problem in his study of the smaller urban centres of Minnesota, for which he devised two indices, one to indicate the functional importance of a town and the other to indicate its specialization. Webb's *functional index* was designed to indicate the importance of a particular function in relation to the general importance of that function in the group of urban settlements being studied. The index was arrived at by taking the percentage of a town's labour force employed in a particular occupation and dividing it by the average percentage in that occupation for the group of urban centres being studied. Thus if an average of 30 per cent was employed in manufacturing, and 60 per cent of the workers in a particular town were employed in that occupation, its functional index for manufacturing was 2. This calculation was repeated for all the urban occupations, and the functions which showed the highest indices were used as the basis for an occupational classification.

To draw attention to the most specialized towns and to summarize the functional indices, a *specialization index* was also calculated. This index was simply the total of the functional indices for all the occupations found in a town divided by 100. In Minnesota the outstanding distinction was between those towns which were small central places, providing retailing and wholesaling services for their surrounding areas and possessing a low specialization index, and those which were manufacturing or mining towns, with a high index and more specialized locations.

All these urban classifications, however, do not make an explicit analysis of the role of urban settlements as central places, which serve hinterlands of varying size and possess services of varying levels of specialization. Indeed geographers have tended to study the classification of towns and cities by occupations and the hierarchy of urban service centres as two completely separate topics, although both are closely connected. This is all the more surprising as presumably the obvious application of most classifications is to allow a more penetrating study of urban locations by drawing attention to the relation between a centre's function and its location; and, in the study of location, the degree to which a town or city possesses specialized tertiary occupations is of clear importance.

In fairness it should be said that statistics of employment provide a very blunt tool for studying urban areas as service centres, and it has often been necessary to adopt different techniques for studying the "urban hierarchy", as it has been called. The focus of interest in this work has not been in urban occupations as such, but the manner in which service activities of varying levels of specialization are grouped in distinctive ways, concentrated in particular cities and command characteristic spheres of influence. It is to the location, size and spacing of cities that attention must now be turned.

Selected Reading

On the economic functioning of cities see

R. U. RATCLIFF, *Urban Land Economics* (New York, 1949), especially chapter 2, The economics of urbanization.

A useful summary of the basic/non-basic idea is provided by

J. W. ALEXANDER, The basic/non-basic concept of urban economic functions, *Economic Geography* **30** (1954), 246–61.

But see also the remarks of V. Roterus and W. Calef:

Notes on the basic/non-basic employment ratio, *Economic Geography* **31** (1955), 17–20.

Many of the classic articles on the urban economic base are collected in

R. W. PFOUTS (ed.), *The Techniques of Urban Economic Analysis* (New York, 1960).

One method of distinguishing the basic population of a city is described in

E. L. ULLMAN and M. F. DACEY, The minimum requirements approach to the urban economic base in K. Norborg (ed.), *Proceedings of the I.G.U. Symposium on Urban Geography, Lund 1960* (Lund, 1962), pp. 121–43.

The complicated inter-relations in the economy of a particular city are described in

R. ARTLE, *Studies in the Structure of the Stockholm Economy* (Stockholm, 1959; American edition, Ithaca, 1965).

A shorter, more general analysis of the same theme is

W. ISARD, R. A. KAVESH and R. E. KUENNE, The economic base and structure of the urban metropolitan region, *American Sociological Review* **18** (1953), 317–21.

Occupational connections in a city are explained in

W. Z. HIRSCH, Interindustry relations of a Metropolitan area, *Review of Economics and Statistics* **41** (1959), 360–9.

See also the input–output table showing inter-industry transactions in Calcutta, provided in

N. K. BOSE, Calcutta: a premature metropolis, *Scientific American* **213**, no. 3 (September 1965), 91–102, table on p. 97.

The urban classifications specifically mentioned in the text are to be found in the following articles:

C. D. HARRIS, A functional classification of cities in the United States, *Geographical Review* **33** (1943), 86–99.

L. L. POWNALL, Functions of New Zealand towns, *Annals of the Association of American Geographers* **43** (1953), 332–50.

H. J. NELSON, A service classification of American cities, *Economic Geography* **31** (1955), 189–210.

W. STEIGENGA, A comparative analysis and a classification of Netherlands towns, *Tijdschrift voor Economische en Sociale Geografie* **46** (1955), 108.

C. A. MOSER and W. SCOTT, *British Towns: a Statistical Study of Their Social and Economic Differences* (London, 1961).

C. D. HARRIS, *Cities of the Soviet Union: studies in their functions, size, density, and growth* (Monograph Series, no. 5, Association of American Geographers, Chicago, 1970).

J. W. MAXWELL, The functional structure of Canadian cities: a classification of cities, *Geographical Bulletin* **7** (1965), 79–104.

J. W. WEBB, Basic concepts in the analysis of small urban centres of Minnesota, *Annals of the Association of American Geographers* **49** (1959), 55–72.

For a penetrating review of much of the literature in the field of urban classification see

R. H. T. SMITH, Method and purpose in functional town classification, *Annals of The Association of American Geographers* **55** (1965), 539–48.

CHAPTER 5

THE LOCATION, SPACING AND SIZE OF URBAN SETTLEMENTS

MANY casual observers have commented on what appears to them the haphazard scatter of towns and cities over the earth's surface. Even to someone who is familiar with the diverse functions provided by urban settlements, the distribution of towns and cities presents a confusing pattern which is difficult to sort out. A first step towards gaining some insight into this matter is made when the various factors behind urban location are isolated. It must, however, be recalled that in practice the influence of each locational factor varies with the mixture of activities found in particular urban settlements.

Factors in the Location of Cities

Putting the problem in its simplest terms, four basic factors lie behind the location of cities. Those settlements which are predominantly concerned with serving the needs of surrounding areas, the so-called "central places", require to be accessible to the people who use them. Secondly, those cities which are concerned with linking an area to the outside world or with certain types of manufacturing are often located on through routes. A third locating factor is provided by highly localized physical resources, on which groups of cities are clustered. Finally, there is often a measure of chance or human whim in urban location, which is often overlooked, simply because this factor is so difficult to assess.

The location of central places is closely connected with the general distribution of population. If the basic population of an area is evenly spread, then the towns which serve it will also be distributed evenly. If, for some reason or another, the distribution of population is uneven, central places will also be spread unevenly, concentrated in locations accessible to the greatest number of people. But some central places in

favourable locations cater for more people and can offer more specialized services. These settlements tend to grow progressively larger, their size depending on their degree of specialization, thus producing various types of central places, characterized by differing populations and zones of influence. Often the resulting hierarchical system exhibits a degree of regularity which has encouraged efforts to formulate generalizations about the distribution and size of central places. Indeed, this matter is so important and has been given so much attention by geographers that it must be returned to later in this chapter.

A second factor governing the location of urban settlements is the distribution of through transport routes and break-of-bulk points along them. Incidental to its primary function, a through transport route often modifies the pattern of local accessibility in an area, since it can hardly fail to have an effect on local transport facilities. As a result a through transport route can distort the central place arrangement of the cities and towns near to it. In Britain, for example, the London to Birmingham motorway, designed to connect two major conurbations, has also had a considerable impact on the local accessibility of towns close to its route.

Transport routes are most influential in governing the location of cities which link regions to external areas. Often the dominating metropolis of a region has had its origin as a transport centre, although later urban growth has attracted so many other functions that this original stimulus to its development has been masked. Many of the great coastal cities of the world provide an example of a location of this kind, lying as they do at the junction of two kinds of transport. But inland cities can also provide examples, a classic case being Chicago, where twenty-one railway systems terminate and meet the Great Lakes waterway.

Urban settlements tend to grow on transport routes only at specific places, particularly at junctions and break-of-bulk points, where one form of transport is changed for another. In fact, there are innumerable locations of this kind—at road and railway junctions, at the head of sea and river navigation, or where a route changes direction and passengers and goods are likely to branch off from one form of transport to another. Hence settlements whose locations are guided by transport routes are found not only at the end of these routes, but also along them. What is important is not the number of routes which come together at a particular point, but the degree to which passengers and goods are interchanged there.

Urban settlements which owe their location to transport facilities possess a variety of functions. Often a line of small local service centres is attracted to a transport route. Or again, some towns mainly provide services for passengers and vehicles moving along transport routes, although settlements of this kind are easiest to pick out in relatively empty areas, where there are no other stimuli for urban growth. Break-of-bulk points are convenient points for certain types of manufacturing, and this in turn provides a reason for urban growth: for example, sugar refining and flour milling are often found at the ports through which the raw materials are imported. A large centre which has been given considerable accessibility by a focus of routes is likely to provide specialized retail and social services; and because of the links such a centre has with the outside world, it is likely to be a focus for wholesale as well as retail trade.

The third factor in the location of cities is the tendency for certain kinds of specialized urban settlements to cluster together. These urban clusters tend to grow around some localized physical resource; and often manufacturing is a dominant occupation. In Britain the cotton manufacturing towns of Lancashire and the woollen towns of Yorkshire provide two examples of this kind of development where a coalfield has been the principal physical resource which located the cluster of towns. Similar examples are common elsewhere in Europe and in parts of the United States.

Some towns whose location was originally governed by physical resources have functions other than manufacturing. Extensive, sandy beaches, for instance, have supported the development of resort towns. An example of this is provided by the string of resorts found along the coast of Lancashire, of which Blackpool is the best known, but which also includes Lytham St. Annes, Bispham and Cleveleys. Or again, tracts of well-drained land with attractive scenery close to a large metropolis may well encourage the growth of a group of commuter settlements. Some of the towns close to London which are associated with the North Downs may be looked upon as an example of this kind of development.

Although physical resources are often important in locating clusters of towns, they are not the only reason for their growth and have not necessarily predestined the precise form which urban development has taken. Even where physical resources were important originally, other factors often become more influential later. Thus coalfields provided power when industrial towns were growing in the nineteenth century and were a greater stimulus to industrial location than they are today, but they did not control the precise form which industrial specialization took. The concentration of pottery manufacture in the group of towns forming Stoke-on-Trent, or of light engineering in and around Birmingham, is difficult to explain convincingly on environmental grounds and the origin of these groups of specialized cities may owe much to fortuitous circumstances. But once started on a particular path, the very existence of a specialist group of towns encourages their further development. Local industries become increasingly intertwined by technological and economic links, making a move elsewhere difficult; and various ancillary services develop which encourage further concentration in these specialized regions.

In the twentieth century the growth of clusters of urban settlements is more frequently found around large metropolises and results in what are sometimes called "city regions". Often these are made up of small country towns and villages which have been drawn into the ambit of a major city and have been enormously expanded as a result. Sometimes this expansion has been undertaken as a result of social policy, as in the "new" and "expanded" towns around London, which have been designed to relocate some of the urban expansion which would otherwise have been associated with the continuous built-up area of the Metropolis.

The towns in these city regions are related to one another by the functions which they perform. Some may form commuter settlements, some may be manufacturing centres, some may be shopping and administrative centres, and some may possess a mixture of functions. But all will be bound together by social and economic links, if not by a continuous built-up area. The groups of towns do not normally show the kind of industrial specialization which was found in nineteenth-century industrial regions, but rather they are dominated by the so-called "light" industries. Often these are industries which profit from being near consumers, and often they draw benefit from being near other industrialists whose products and services they use.

This kind of clustering is perhaps best exemplified by the urban development along the north-eastern seaboard of the United States. Here rather special circumstances exist, since there is not one major city, but a line of ports which have spawned other towns around them. The most important factor, however, is the tendency for modern industrial cities to form clusters, and this has produced in this region the most extensive, highly-urbanized area in the world.

Finally there is always likely to be a measure of whim and chance in urban location. Although it may be assumed that in numerous cases the detailed location of an urban settlement was guided by the chance decisions of individuals, it is difficult to unearth specific evidence. Often even the date of the foundation of historic cities is lost in antiquity, not to mention any knowledge of the forces which guided the original choice of location. Even in areas where urban settlements have been founded in the nineteenth century, evidence is difficult to untangle, since the factors influencing their original foundation are often hidden by developments which follow immediately afterwards.

For example, a town may be located on a transport route for some quite fortuitous reason, but, once established, the very presence of a nucleus of population and certain urban services tends to encourage further growth if there are no competitors in the vicinity. Such a town may well attract additional transport routes and thus add further to its nodality and the chance of its growth. Once an urban settlement has been firmly established, the fixed capital it represents will create a vested interest against any change of location; and in any case modern social and economic trends encourage continued urban prosperity and growth.

Madison, Wisconsin, provides an interesting example of the actual factors which influenced the founding of an individual city. At first sight the location of this city, on what now seems an accessible and attractive site, seems a good instance of the role of the physical environment; but the history of the choice of site reveals that other forces were at work. In 1836 the Wisconsin Territorial Legislature was obliged to choose a site for a permanent capital. A total of sixteen localities were considered, all of them owned by speculators, who energetically advanced the claims of their own land. The decision to locate the capital on its present site was taken by 15 votes to 11, and this decision owed more to intrigue by the most subtle of the speculators than to any careful assessment of site and situation.*

Whim and chance, however, are more important in governing the location of individual settlements than in forming the regional pattern of urban development. Indeed, most cities show the operation in varying proportions of all four forces discussed briefly here. The more functions which a group of cities has, the more likely it is that a mixture of factors has influenced their location and the more difficult it is to sort them out. Nevertheless, to analyse the location of cities in terms of these possibilities helps towards the understanding of what at first sight may appear to be a haphazard scatter of towns, although it may not allow a precise statement of the relative importance of these various factors.

Urban Zones of Influence

The location and spacing of towns and cities clearly owes much to the manner in which individual urban settlements are linked to places outside their own limits. As a result considerable attention has been given to the delimitation of the areas joined by social and economic bonds to a

* For an account see J. W. Alexander, An economic base study of Madison, Wisconsin, *Wisconsin Commerce Papers* 1, no. 4 (1953), appendix B.

particular urban settlement. Although an approach of this kind can be applied to the study of a city's manufacturing activities, this mode of analysis is most appropriate for its service activities and produces clearest results for settlements which predominantly function as service centres (or central places).

The area linked socially and economically to an urban settlement has been given various names. Some geographers have adopted the German term "Hinterland", originally applied to the region served by a port. Others have felt that "Umland" would be linguistically more accurate, particularly for inland towns which have dealings in all directions; but unfortunately this term has also been applied to the immediate environs of a town as well as to the larger area served by it. A. E. Smailes has coined the graphic expression "urban field", drawing an analogy from the study of magnetism; but the comparison is not exact and it is perhaps dangerous to rely on a term from another scientific discipline, since the relations between towns and their surroundings do not operate with the regularity of a physical law. Other expressions like "sphere of influence", "zone of influence", "tributary area" or "catchment area" have also been used, although they are not without their difficulties. The area influenced by a town is a two-dimensional feature, not a sphere, nor does it necessarily form a continuous zone. For that matter, goods and services flow both into and out of a town: most modern urban settlements and their hinterlands are economically interdependent, rather than one being a tributary to the other.

The precise term used matters little, provided that it is not taken as an exact description of the relationship between an urban settlement and its surroundings. More important are the reasons for delimiting zones of influence at all. An analysis of the rural area served by a market town gives some indication of the relations between town and country, which is of practical application in examining the provision of goods and services in an urban centre. As smaller towns fall within the areas served by larger cities, the delimitation of urban zones of influence also sheds light on the manner in which a city at a particular level in the urban hierarchy provides specialist services for the surrounding population, both rural and urban. Finally, very large cities extend a particularly intensive influence over the areas around them, so much so that they can be said to organize their hinterlands, thus forming functional regions. Thus the analysis of the hinterlands of metropolitan cities has implications for the general study of regional geography.

In examining zones of influence one is immediately brought up against the practical difficulty of obtaining readily available information. Studies of individual towns usually rest upon laborious personal

field-work. One commonly adopted method, for example, is to establish
on a map the areas served by shops, by schools, and by other urban
activities which are typical of a town at that level of specialization
(Fig. 22). This method of analysis is applicable to cities and towns at
all levels in the urban hierarchy. A. E. Smailes, for example, used it

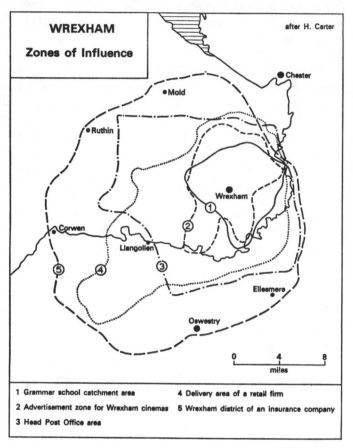

WREXHAM

Zones of Influence

after H. Carter

1 Grammar school catchment area
2 Advertisement zone for Wrexham cinemas
3 Head Post Office area
4 Delivery area of a retail firm
5 Wrexham district of an insurance company

Fig. 22. The zones of influence of Wrexham. (*Source*: Carter, *The Towns
of Wales* (1966), p. 123.)

effectively in his study of the zone of influence of Ballymena, a town of
some 14,000 people which is located in Co. Antrim, Northern Ireland.
To delimit the zone served by this settlement he depended upon such
features as the area served by buses leaving Ballymena after 9 p.m., the
region in which the local weekly newspaper circulated, as well as the
tributary area of the town's shops and secondary schools. As a result he

was able to show that the air of busy prosperity for which this town is locally famous owes much to the fact that it serves in one way or another a population of over 65,000 people.* In other words, there are almost four times as many customers outside the town as within it. At a higher level in the urban hierarchy the criteria used reflect the more specialized nature of the distinctive functions of larger settlements and employ information like the area served by a city's banking and insurance facilities, the circulation of its daily newspapers, its accessibility by rail, and the areas from which both weekly and more occasional shoppers are drawn.

Studies of this kind use information gathered in the urban settlement itself and, as it were, look outwards from a city towards its surroundings. H. E. Bracey has inverted this method by examining the countryside independently of the town. By making a questionnaire survey in parts of southern England, he has built up urban zones of influence by listing for each village the urban services provided by various nearby towns and mapping the results (Fig. 23). Admittedly, as it stands, the method is limited in its application, since it requires a settlement pattern in which villages house a high proportion of the rural population. It is also best adapted to examining the spheres of influence of small towns directly concerned with serving surrounding rural areas. Yet in spite of these restrictions the method also has some advantages. In particular it focuses attention on those aspects of a town's social and economic provision which are expressly designed for the surrounding rural population. Thus the method is particularly well suited for examining the role of a relative small urban settlement as a central place, serving a rural community. The system also has the practical advantage of avoiding the necessity of obtaining information from busy and often reticent shopkeepers. As with the other methods, however, a considerable amount of field-work and other enquiries are required to produce a satisfactory result.

As a result a number of short cuts have been devised to gather information about the limits of urban zones of influence. The usual method is to take only one index, which is particularly expressive of the links of a town or city with its surroundings. One well-known example of this approach is the use of the circulation areas of daily newspapers to indicate the zone of influence of metropolitan centres. Such a mode of analysis is most applicable where these cities are relatively widely spaced and where a whole country is not dominated by national newspapers, as is the case in Britain. Hence this method has been used effectively in the United States (in particular by R. E. Park, one of the pioneers of urban studies), where the information of the Audit Bureau

* A. E. Smailes, *The Geography of Towns* (London, 1953), pp. 150–3.

of Circulation provides an easily accessible source for the whole country.

The choice of a daily newspaper as a single index has more advantages than mere convenience. The newspaper brings its readers into constant contact with the metropolis, its advertising provides information about goods and services available in the city, its opinion column disseminates

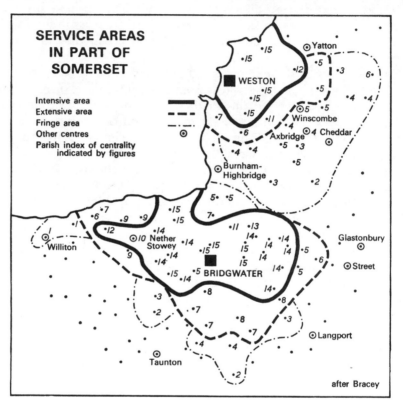

Fig. 23. Intensive, extensive and fringe areas of Weston-super-Mare and Bridgwater. (*Source*: Bracey, *Transactions of the Institute of British Geographers* no. 19 (1953), 99.)

the metropolitan political outlook (or at least one expression of it), and the selection of news tends to build up a community of interest within the metropolitan hinterland. This newspaper circulation serves as an index of some of the social ties between a city and its hinterland as well of some of the economic links. Indeed, the newspaper itself has been an important factor in strengthening these connections, although today a local television station may provide a similar service.

Small local newspapers, which are published only once or twice a week, can also be used in the same way to measure the influence of settlements much lower in the urban hierarchy. For example, J. P. Haughton has studied the circulation of local newspapers in Eire in an attempt to delimit the zones of influence of country towns (Fig. 24). Details of the circulation areas of these newspapers are more difficult to obtain and, working at this scale, more detail is required. As a result, Haughton used internal evidence within the newspapers, in particular the extent of news coverage and the area from which local advertisements were placed, as the main line of evidence.

Another method of delimiting the zones of influence of small urban centres has been devised for Britain by F. H. W. Green. Green used local bus timetables as the basis of his analysis, making the assumption that towns are also usually bus centres, that is, places having at least one scheduled route which operates on market days during the winter months. Green defined the hinterland of a bus centre as the area within which it is the most accessible centre. Access to a town during the 1940's (when the method was devised) was provided for most people by public transport; and so the bus hinterland was assumed to bear a close relationship to the zone of influence of the retail and other services provided by small towns. The mapping of other indexes for a number of random examples has shown that Green's method gave a good approximation to the zone of influence of most British towns. When applied to other countries it has proved a less satisfactory method; and, of course, the more general diffusion of the private ownership of motor-cars since the method was devised has reduced its applicability.

Even after careful personal field-work a map of the various zones of influence around a town almost invariably shows a lack of exact correspondence among the various boundaries recorded. Partly this is a result of fortuitous circumstances, like, for example, the manner in which a school bus service is operated, or the way in which local library services have been provided. Often, too, not all the criteria chosen exhibit a similar level of specialization: some services may tap only the immediate environs of a town, while others may have no competition for many miles. But even working at the same level of specialization the hinterlands associated with various commercial activities will vary as a result of the differing enterprise of individual shopkeepers, since the more efficient shops will normally reach a wider area and will compete more effectively with retail outlets located in villages. At best, then, even with the most careful selection of criteria, all that can be achieved is a belt of lines running around an urban settlement, which will indicate

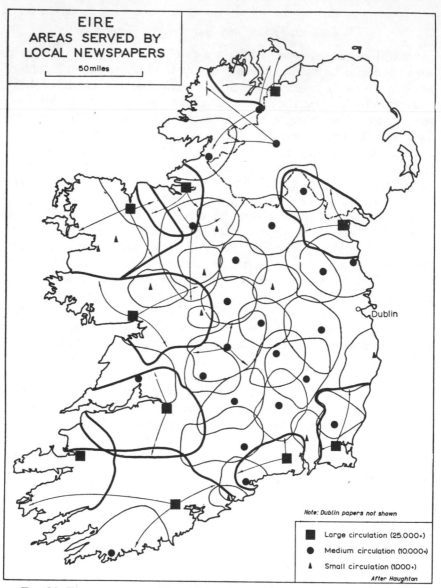

EIRE
AREAS SERVED BY
LOCAL NEWSPAPERS
50 miles

Dublin

Note: Dublin papers not shown

■ Large circulation (25,000+)
● Medium circulation (10,000+)
▲ Small circulation (1000+)

After Haughton

Fig. 24. Eire: areas served by local newspapers. (*Source*: Haughton, *Irish Geography* **2**, no. 2 (1950), 53.)

On this map the area where a particular newspaper circulates is enclosed by a line. In eastern and central Ireland only newspapers serving small localities can survive in competition with Dublin papers, which are not shown in this map but which serve all of the Irish Republic. Away from the immediate influence of Dublin, local newspapers with more extensive circulations can survive, particularly in the west. Their zones of influence also overlap the territories of smallest papers, so that there are approximately three levels in the hierarchy of newspaper distribution.

quite clearly the general rural areas served by a town, but not its precise limits (Fig. 22).

A further difficulty is revealed when the hinterlands of all the towns in an area are put together on the one map. This often shows considerable overlap of hinterlands, which represents no chance occurrence, but is often the normal state of affairs, particularly in a highly urbanized country where transport is relatively flexible and towns are close together. Thus around any sizable town there is a zone where it experiences little or no competition from neighbouring centres. Farther out from the town its influence falls away until an area is reached which is completely dominated by other centres. H. E. Bracey's work in Somerset has allowed him to study the nature of this overlap in some detail. By measuring the intensity of the urban influence in the county as it is experienced in villages, he has shown that the decrease of influence from an urban centre is not a gradual one (Fig. 23). First, there is a relatively sharp break from the high intensity to a concentric band where trade is divided between two towns. Taking the range of services as a whole the inhabitants of this intermediate zone use the competing towns equally. Then there is another abrupt drop in intensity to another belt, which is sometimes discontinuous. Here there are only tenuous affiliations to the central town and most business is done elsewhere.

Further complications arise in heavily industrialized regions, where towns have been established for purposes other than providing for the nearby rural population. In practice it is rare for such a town not to build up some relationships with its immediate surroundings, but the circumstances of the town's industrial origins are likely to affect the nature of its zone of influence. Clearly its tributary area will be much more restricted than that of a town of equal size, which has grown as a market centre. While a service centre which has grown to serve the rural population will dominate a relatively clearly defined area, an intrusive industrial town may well not have the full range of urban services appropriate to its size. These missing functions will be supplied from other centres, thus making its zone of influence less clearly defined (Fig. 25). There is some evidence, too, that the zone of influence of such a centre is less able to resist competition from other towns, if only because it is likely to be a more unattractive place to visit on a weekly shopping expedition.

It will be clear that the analysis of urban zones of influence is most appropriate for those cities whose dominant role is that of serving as a central place, although most settlements of any reasonable size will have this among their various functions. Certain specialized cities, however, present inherent difficulties in that they have grossly distorted or non-contiguous zones of influence. Some urban settlements which owe their *raison d'être* to extractive industry form a difficult class. Kuwait, for example, is concerned with supplying oil to a distant market and the zone of influence for this dominant function is discontinuous and far removed. Other cities have curious zones of influence as a result of political factors: West Berlin serves certain functions for the German

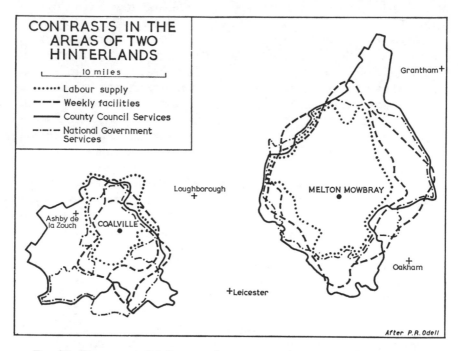

Fig. 25. The zones of influence of two contrasting towns. (*Source*: Odell, *Transactions of the Institute of British Geographers*, no. 23 (1957), 180.)

Melton Mowbray is an ancient market town; and although it has recently acquired more manufacturing industry, it still retains very strong ties with its rural surroundings. Coalville has grown in the last 100 years as a coal-mining centre. Its services originally developed to serve its own population, although the town has now established rather more tenuous links with surrounding areas.

Federal Republic, but it is detached from its zone of influence by political boundaries, and the precise economic bonds which exist are extremely artificial. Certain holiday resorts present similar difficulties of analysis, since they have few real links with their immediate surroundings and may serve people who live many miles away. Las Vegas, with its dependence on transient trade, is perhaps an extreme example of the difficulties of studying effective zones of influence, but difficulties of this kind apply to all towns of this type.

The Hinterlands of a Metropolis

Even when these extreme cases are discounted, the larger the city, the more complicated are its relations with its surroundings, since not only does a large city provide certain characteristic services for its region, but it also provides the services of a major town and a village for progressively more restricted areas. As a result the large city is surrounded by a series of hinterlands, which reflect the varying levels of specialization exhibited by its shops, industries and institutions.

As long ago as 1930, R. E. Dickinson recognized three composite zones around Leeds and Bradford. First, there was the Yorkshire Region, linked to these two central cities by social, economic and cultural bonds. Inside that belt was the outer suburban and commuting zone of the conurbation, with daily links with the centre. Finally there was the continuous built-up area of the conurbation, which was looked upon as forming a central zone. Working in greater detail, Huguette Vivian has made the same observation in her study of the regional relations of Grenoble. The national influence of Grenoble depends on its specialized manufacturing, on certain branches of learning found in its university and on its role as a centre for the French Alpine recreational economy; but it also serves as a central place for the surrounding region.

Going outwards from the centre, Grenoble serves its region at a number of levels of intensity (Fig. 26). First there are its suburbs, which includes the fringe of the built-up area and some adjacent municipalities. Here the contacts with Grenoble proper are intimate and daily. The population of this zone looks to the central city for shopping, factory employment, school attendance and its remaining rural areas are used for market gardening for the city. This zone is being inexorably absorbed into the built-up area of Grenoble. Surrounding this belt are the "environs" of Grenoble. Here the urbanized area is no longer continuous, but the influence of the central city is still very strong. Transport services to the centre are frequent and the network of routes is dense. The inhabitants of this zone, too, depend exclusively on Grenoble for educational services; and although they obtain their day-to-day purchases locally they resort to the city for any major items. The environs grade into what Vivian has called the "vicinity". Here smaller towns have developed local centres of commerce and industry, but Grenoble provides the more specialized services: the central city, for example, dominates wholesale trade, secondary education and medical services. The outer limit of the vicinity is approximately demarcated by about an hour's travelling time from the central city. As a result this belt is also the outer zone contributing daily commuters to the central city. Because of its accessibility it is also the area used for week-end outings from Grenoble and for family recreation.

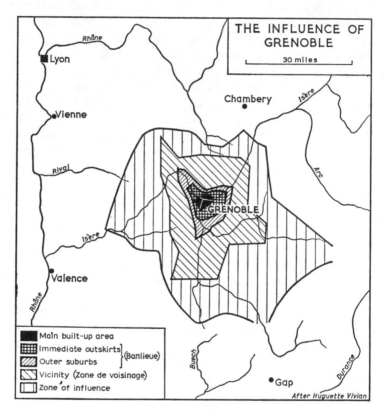

FIG. 26. The zones of influence of Grenoble. (*Source*: Vivian, *Revue de Géographie Alpine* **47** (1959), 545.)

In the immediate outskirts of Grenoble contact with the central city is intimate and daily; in the outer suburbs day-to-day purchases are obtained locally; in the vicinity of the city local centres of commerce and industry have developed, although there are also many daily commuters to the city; finally in the outer zone of influence contact is less frequent and is limited to more specialized services.

Finally Grenoble is surrounded by what might be called its zone of influence. Here the city is no longer the place of work or regular shopping of any significant proportion of the population. It remains, however, the centre from which a daily newspaper is published and the headquarters from which professional representatives operate. Higher education and specialist medical services for this zone are also provided from Grenoble. The extent of the "zone of influence" is controlled by the distribution of other large urban settlements. To the north-east in the direction of Chambéry, to the north-west towards Lyons, and to the south-west towards Valence, the zone of influence extends some 15 miles. But to the south-east, where there are no competing settlements, it reaches 50 to 60 miles into the mountain valleys of Dauphiné.

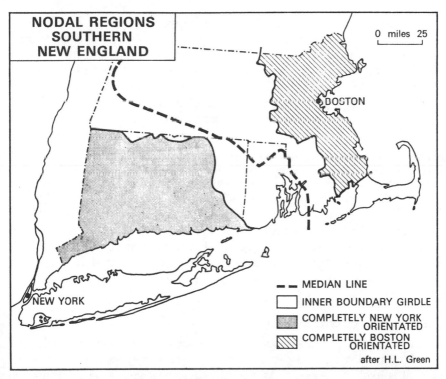

NODAL REGIONS
SOUTHERN
NEW ENGLAND

0   miles   25

BOSTON

NEW YORK

- - MEDIAN LINE
☐ INNER BOUNDARY GIRDLE
▨ COMPLETELY NEW YORK ORIENTATED
▧ COMPLETELY BOSTON ORIENTATED

after H.L. Green

FIG. 27. Nodal regions in southern New England. (*Source*: Green, *Economic Geography* **31** (1955), 299.)

This map summarizes the results of applying seven criteria to the analysis of the zones of influence of Boston and New York in southern New England. The criteria used included the organization of banking, the addresses of directors of firms located in the two cities, the origins of telephone calls, the circulation of daily newspapers, the destination of railway passengers, the limits of winter commuter traffic, and the home addresses of holiday visitors.

Beyond these limits the influence of Grenoble diminishes sharply, and its role as a metropolitan centre is superseded by other centres, except where it offers unique services as a centre for certain modern industries, for certain branches of learning in its university and as the focus of the French Alpine recreational economy.

The zones of influence of metropolitan centres are of general importance from a number of points of view. The gradual rise of these areas of metropolitan dominance in the nineteenth and twentieth centuries has stamped a new geographical pattern on many countries and is now a force to be taken into account in the regional geography of some countries. Because large cities tend to organize the areas around them, both socially and economically, they can be said to form nodal or functional regions.

An example of this kind of influence is given by H. L. Green's study of the hinterlands of New York and Boston (Fig. 27). The expanding urban areas of these two conurbations and their growing influence in the area between them has made southern New England distinctive from the rest of the region. The delimitation of metropolitan regions of this kind may also have some practical importance. As long ago as 1917, C. B. Fawcett delimited the "provinces" of England, which were essentially the hinterlands of major metropolitan centres. It was suggested that these "provinces" might well provide a more logical basis for regional administration than the English counties and county boroughs. The relevance of these ideas has been enhanced by the various *ad hoc* administrative regions which have been established in Britain during recent decades, and which now form a complex and not always functionally perfect system. A case can be made out for the use of metropolitan hinterlands as standard administrative regions, which would serve the needs of regional land-use planning as well as those of many of the nationalized industries and other organs of government.

The Urban Hierarchy

The discussion of urban zones of influence will have made it clear that the larger a city, the wider the range of services, goods and functions that it is likely to provide. As a result, there has been a parallel interest among geographers in the classification of cities according to the specialization of their services. Such studies largely began as descriptive exercises, but underlying this work has been the thought that the information would have practical utility. In particular, an implicit idea was that the existing hierarchy of towns and cities would form a useful basis for the organization of the growing administrative machine of the

State. There has also been a concern among geographers to establish the precise relationship between the size of a settlement, measured in terms of its population, and the range of services which it offers. This, too, has immediate practical applications in planning, but much of this work has been used to provide essential data for the development of quite abstract theories concerning the logical size and distribution of central places.

An early British study in the descriptive classification of service centres was R. E. Dickinson's analysis of East Anglian towns, which he classified into four grades, using such criteria as the turnover of their livestock markets and the presence of banking facilities, secondary schools and cinemas. Later, A. E. Smailes refined these criteria and applied them to all of England and Wales. His starting point was the recognition of "fully-fledged" towns, which had achieved a certain minimum provision of retail shopping, possessed certain basic financial services and provided local *foci* for social, educational and recreational activities. These general requirements were translated into specific criteria, so that to be classified as a "town" an urban settlement needed to possess at least three banks, a Woolworth's store, a secondary school, a hospital, a cinema and a weekly newspaper. Conveniently enough, these facilities tended to occur together, so that it was possible to speak of the "trait complex" of a fully-fledged English town.

Other levels of specialization were recognized in the same way. For example, settlements which did not possess this full range of urban services were classified as "sub-towns" and "urban villages". On the other hand, a "city" had all the services of a town and also possessed department stores, an evening newspaper and specialized hospital services. A "major city" had, in addition, the regional headquarters of both government departments and private firms; and, at the time this work was being carried out, a major city in England was also made distinctive by its civic university and its daily morning newspaper. Work similar to this was undertaken elsewhere, in such diverse countries as Germany, the United States and India, the criteria used being modified in relation to the particular social and economic context of the local area.

In all these studies central places were grouped into distinct categories, so that it was possible to speak of an urban hierarchy, with settlements at one level of specialization being clearly distinguished from those at the next level. The question arises, however, whether a hierarchy exists in reality or whether these distinct categories have simply been produced by the various methods of classification used. In other words, does reality consist of a continuum of various-sized urban settlements with no clear functional breaks between them, or do central places fall naturally into distinct categories?

Some experimental studies of small areas have recently been carried out to test these points. For example, B. J. L. Berry and W. L. Garrison have identified a hierarchical system of central places in Snohomish county, Washington, by showing statistically that the urban settlements in the county fall into three groups, measured in terms of the number of functions which they possess. Again, Berry has recognized discrete hierarchies in south-western Iowa, using the statistical technique of factor analysis on the results of a questionnaire survey. But although urban hierarchies can be demonstrated in small areas, the task becomes more difficult when larger regions are studied, since then manufacturing industry complicates the general distribution of population, and local social and economic differences produce detailed variations in the nature of the hierarchy, thus making it much more difficult to produce a general finding.

In those areas where a hierarchical system of cities and their associated zones of influence are fully developed there is a considerable degree of regularity to be found. Often there seems to be a constant ratio between the number of cities at one level in the urban hierarchy and the number at the next level, with the zones of influence of the more specialized cities being superimposed in a regular fashion upon those of central places.

The generalizations require certain assumptions to be made. They assume an area that is without geographical variations in its topography or primary production, and one that is also without limits like the seacoast. They also imply a highly developed system of transportation which will allow cities to compete with one another, so that their hinterlands are contiguous and a hierarchical system of urban settlements can develop fully. Although this complete range of conditions is rarely found in reality, the study of the theoretical arrangement of central places is not without value, since it allows a clearer understanding of the relationships which exist between town and country and between towns at various levels in the urban hierarchy. In addition, the existence of an ideal model of the arrangement of service centres helps to focus attention on those departures from the "normal" which are found when real situations are studied. The discrepancy between model and reality poses immediate problems for further research.

Central Place Theory

The most famous generalization is that associated with the German geographer, Walter Christaller. In its simplest terms Christaller's scheme proposed that towns with the lowest level of specialization would be equally spaced and surrounded by hexagonally shaped hinterlands. For every six of these towns there would be a larger, more specialized city which, in turn, would be situated an equal distance from other cities with the same level of specialization as itself. Such a city would also have a larger hexagonal service area for its own specialized services. Even more specialized settlements would also have their own hinterlands and be located at an equal distance from each other. According to Christaller the smallest centres were likely to be located 7 kilometres apart. Centres of the next order of specialization were thought to serve three times the area and three times the population. Hence they would be located 12 kilometres apart ($\sqrt{3} \times 7$). Similarly, the area of the hinterlands of centres at the next level of specialization would again be three times larger (Table 2, Fig. 28).

TABLE 2. THE URBAN HIERARCHY IN SOUTH-WEST GERMANY
(AFTER CHRISTALLER)

Settlement form	Distance apart (km)	Population	Tributary area size (km²)	Population
Market hamlet (Markort)	7	800	45	2,700
Township centre (Amtsort)	12	1,500	135	8,100
County seat (Kreistadt)	21	3,500	400	24,000
District city (Bezirksstadt)	36	9,000	1,200	75,000
Small state capital (Gaustadt)	62	27,000	3,600	225,000
Provincial head capital (Provinzhaupstadt)	108	90,000	10,800	675,000
Regional capital city (Landeshaupstadt)	186	300,000	32,400	2,025,000

Source: E. L. Ullman, *Amer. Jour. Sociology* **46** (1941), 857.

This kind of arrangement has been called a $k = 3$ hierarchy, in which the number of centres at successively less specialized levels in the urban hierarchy follows a geometric progression (1, 3, 9, 27, . . .). A hierarchy with these features exhibits what Christaller has called the "marketing principle", with the most important factor influencing the distribution of urban settlements being the need for central places to be as near as possible to the customers they serve. Other hierarchies are also possible: for example, Christaller has suggested that where the cost of the traffic network is important a $k = 4$ hierarchy may be expected, or where administrative control is decisive a $k = 7$ hierarchy is more likely. It is, however, the marketing principle which can be most easily distinguished, and which has had most influence on later workers.

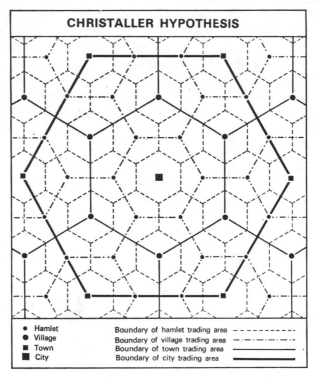

CHRISTALLER HYPOTHESIS

● Hamlet	Boundary of hamlet trading area	– – – – – – – – –
● Village	Boundary of village trading area	– · – · – · – · – ·
■ Town	Boundary of town trading area	——————
■ City	Boundary of city trading area	━━━━━━━

Fig. 28. W. Christaller's theory of the arrangement of trade centres.

In this system there is a constant ratio between the number of trade centres at various levels of specialization and between the areas of their respective zones of influence.

Following Christaller's original work there have been various attempts to refine his ideas, one of the most interesting being the scheme proposed by the German economist August Lösch. Lösch again used hexagonal service areas as the basic units in his theoretical landscape, but allowed various hexagonal systems to coexist (Fig. 29). The resulting arrangement does not produce the "tiered" system of urban centres suggested by Christaller, but leads, more or less, to a continuum of various-sized towns and cities. One result of this work has been a controversy on whether a fixed or a variable relationship exists between centres of differ-ing levels of specialization. At present the view seems to be that, al-though the more complex geometric forms which Lösch postulates as an

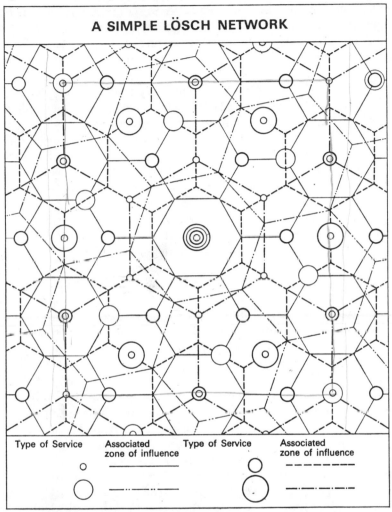

FIG. 29. A simple version of A. Lösch's theory of the arrangement of trade centres. (*Source*: simplified from a diagram in Isard, *Location and Space Economy* (1956), p. 270.)

Hexagonal service areas are again assumed, with distinctive-sized zones of influence for different types of services. Here, however, there is no constant ratio between the various sizes of hexagonal service areas; so that they do not "nest" in the manner characteristic of Christaller's system.

"ideal" arrangement of service centres appears to represent reality more closely, Christaller's model is simpler to grasp and allows a more satisfying discussion of the economic relationships between different orders of settlements. In any case, as interest among some geographers is turning increasingly to the analysis of the geometry of the patterns formed by services centres and their hinterlands, the rather simpler Christaller model is more susceptible to analysis of this kind, and has been given greater attention.

A further development has been the study of two factors controlling the distribution of central places, which were clearly implied in Christaller's original work, but which have now been more explicitly examined, particularly by W. L. Garrison and B. J. L. Berry. One of these factors has been called the "range of a good", which is the distance over which people are prepared to travel to obtain a particular service. The other is the "threshold", which is the minimum amount of purchasing power necessary to support the supply of a particular "good" (or service) from a central place. The range of a particular service from an urban centre has an upper limit, which is determined by competition from other places which supply the same service. The range also has a lower limit, controlled by the threshold necessary to allow it to function.

As a result of the operation of these two factors it is logical to expect a hierarchy of central places. More specialized services require a larger threshold, but also have a more extensive range. Hence they are found in those larger settlements which provide enough purchasers to support them, drawn both from their own populations and from that of their extensive zones of influence. Large centres also provide less specialized services, but as these services have a smaller range, it is also possible for smaller settlements, lying between the larger centres, to compete effectively. Although each individual service may have a unique range and threshold, in practice it must be provided from an urban centre where groups of services are concentrated. As a result distinctive groups of services will develop in those settlements which provide approximately the correct threshold for their survival, within the range (or zone of influence) appropriate for these services.

As might be expected, certain theoretical and practical objections have been raised against Christaller's model of the distribution of central places. It can be argued that overlapping hinterlands are the normal state of affairs in any country with well-developed means of transport, although Christaller made the assumption that the hinterlands of towns of similar specialization do not overlap. There is evidence, too, that the presence of a large urban centre tends to discourage the growth of smaller, less specialized settlements nearby, at what would be the appropriate distance according to Christaller's model. There has also been disagreement about the ratio of smaller centres to settlements at the next level in the urban hierarchy. Another ground for criticism lies in the fact that it is difficult to devise a realistic pattern of communications which would allow an arrangement of superimposed hexagonal hinterlands to function.

When the theoretical scheme is tested against reality additional difficulties emerge. The provision of services does not take place solely from towns which were specifically founded as service centres. Industrial towns, which began their existence without in any way providing for the wants of the surrounding countryside, often develop this function later, thus giving a distorted arrangement of central services. Perhaps this might be looked upon as a special case, which would always be difficult to embody in any theoretical scheme, but in a highly industrialized country it is an important element in understanding the distribution of tertiary activities. One further practical difficulty has theoretical implications. All urban settlements have grown up as a result of an historical process, often in a whole series of different technological situations. But towns founded in the past do not disappear—they continue to function in the present landscape. The American geographer, John Brush, recognized this fact in his study of south-west Wisconsin. Here the first settlements were built when the most common means of transport was by horses and wagon. When railways were built, larger centres developed along the tracks, in some cases on the sites of earlier settlements; and the motor-car is now encouraging the relative growth of other settlements. But the past means of transport can still be picked out in the distribution of the small service centres of this region.

As a result, discrepancies can be expected between the theoretical and the actual distribution of central places, even in areas where physical geography has not had an important influence on the distribution of population. These discrepancies do not necessarily invalidate discussions of central place theory, which are basically concerned with location of service centres in a hypothetical situation where only economic factors are operating. What they do stress is that much of this theory refers to conditions in the Western world in the twentieth century; and there is every reason to believe that details of the theory will be altered in different technological and economic contexts.

Central place theory considers the size of cities as well as their spacing, but there is another generalization which has been made about city size. This is the so-called "rank–size rule", which states that, if all the urban settlements in an area are ranked in descending order of population size, the population of the nth town will be $\frac{1}{n}$ the size of the largest city, and the population of the other urban settlements will be arranged according to the series 1, $\frac{1}{2}$, $\frac{1}{3}$, $\frac{1}{4}$, . . ., $\frac{1}{n}$. When plotted on a graph this produces the result shown on Fig. 30, while an actual

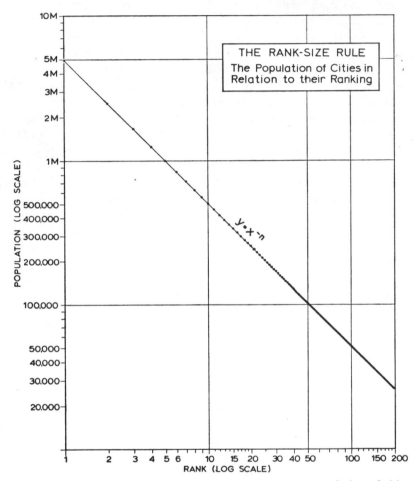

Fig. 30. The rank–size rule: the hypothetical size of the population of cities in relation to their ranking.

example is provided by **Fig. 31**, which shows the sizes of urban settlements in England and Wales in 1961.

The rank–size rule differs in its conception from central place theory. Although Christaller may have been stimulated by the geography of a real area, his central place theory is basically concerned with producing a theoretical model of what reality should be like, given certain basic assumptions. The rank–size rule, on the other hand, is simply an empirical observation, based on the study of actual population statistics and without any theoretical pretensions. As a result, detailed discrepancies abound from country to country—for example, the size of the largest

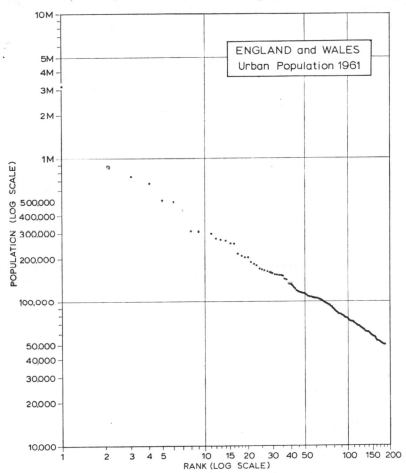

Fig. 31. The size and ranking of urban areas in England and Wales, 1961.

The diagram is based on the population of the administrative areas of towns and cities as shown in the 1961 census. A comparison with Fig. 30 shows that the population of London is greater than the rank–size rule suggests it should be (and, in fact, the population of the total built-up area was much larger than that of the Administrative County of London, shown here). Although the trend of the remaining urban settlements accords roughly with the rule, there are some clear breaks in the slope of the graph, which in any case is rather less steep than the rank–size rule suggests it should be.

city is often greater than the rule suggests it should be. Yet although they are different in conception, there is clearly a large measure of convergence between the two ideas, since both imply a situation in which there are many small cities, a lesser number of medium-sized cities and fewer large cities.

There is, however, one important discrepancy: Christaller's urban hierarchy would produce a stepped arrangement of urban sizes, while the rank–size rule implies a smooth progression of population size from rank to rank. In fact, this discrepancy is more apparent than real. The rank–size rule works best when a large area is being studied, while the urban hierarchy is most clearly seen in reality where a small non-manufacturing area is under study. The discrepancy is thus largely a matter of scale, so that when a whole country is being considered the presence of manufacturing regions and the detailed variation of the urban hierarchy from area to area because of different technological and economic situations hides the breaks in population numbers between different levels of the urban hierarchy. In other words, there is a "random" element which blurs the edges of the hierarchical system of central places and produces a relatively smooth population curve.

Indeed, W. Bunge has claimed that the rank–size rule is a most important confirmation of Christaller's urban hierarchy, since this observation was made independently of discussions of central place theory and approaches the problem from a different point of view. It can be argued that central place theory provides the most convincing explanation of why the population of cities follows the rank–size rule, provided that the presence of a "random" element is accepted.* If this view is correct (and the matter is still open to debate), it stresses the importance of the function of cities as central places in controlling their general size.

Further Reading

A classic discussion of the location of cities is

C. D. Harris and E. L. Ullman, The nature of cities, *Annals of the American Academy of Political and Social Science* **242** (1945), 7–17.

Features of modern city regions are discussed in

M. J. Wise, The city region, *Advancement of Science* **23** (1966), 571–88.

A work covering many of the aspects of the relationships between cities and their surroundings is

R. E. Dickinson, *City and Region: a Geographical Interpretation* (London, 1964).

---

* This point is argued most clearly in M. J. Beckman, City hierarchies and the distribution of city size, *Economic Development and Cultural Change*, **6** (1958), 243–8.

An important bibliography is

B. L. J. BERRY and A. PRED, *Central Place Studies: Bibliography and Review* (Philadelphia, 1961).

The best summary of the features of central places and their associated zones of influence is

B. J. L. BERRY, *Geography of Market Centres and Retail Distribution* (Englewood Cliffs, 1967).

A pioneer study in Britain concerned with the influence of urban settlements on their surroundings is

A. E. SMAILES, The analysis and delimitation of urban fields, *Geography* **32** (1947), 151–61.

An example of H. E. Bracey's work is found in his article

Towns as rural service centres: an index of centrality with special reference to Somerset, *Transactions of the Institute of British Geographers* no. 19 (1953), 95–105. See also H. E. BRACEY, *Social Provision in Rural Wiltshire* (London, 1958).

On the use of newspaper circulations as indices of urban zones of influence see

R. E. PARK and C. NEWCOMB, Newspaper circulation and metropolitan regions, in R. D. MCKENZIE, *The Metropolitan Community* (New York, 1933), chapter 8.
J. P. HAUGHTON, Irish local newspapers: a geographical study, *Irish Geography* **2,** no. 2 (1950), 52–7.

An example of F. H. W. Green's method of studying bus services is given in his article

Urban hinterlands in England and Wales: an analysis of bus services, *Geographical Journal* **96** (1950), 64–81.

See also Green's appraisal of his method in the light of modern transport conditions in

Urban hinterlands: fifteen years on, *Geographical Journal* **132** (1966), 263–6.

For a comparison of the zones of influence of a market and an industrial town see

P. R. ODELL, The hinterlands of Melton Mowbray and Coalville, *Transactions of the Institute of British Geographers* no. 23 (1957), 175–90.

The zones of influence of larger settlements are analysed in

H. VIVIAN, La zone d'influence régionale de Grenoble, *Revue de Géographie Alpine* **47** (1959), 539–83.
R. E. DICKINSON, The regional functions and zones of influence of Leeds and Bradford, *Geography* **15** (1930), 548–57.
H. L. GREEN, Hinterland boundaries of New York City and Boston in southern New England, *Economic Geography* **31** (1955), 283–300.

An early study of the urban hierarchy is

R. E. DICKINSON, The distribution and functions of the smaller urban settlements of East Anglia, *Geography* **7** (1932), 19–31.

All of England and Wales is covered in

A. E. SMAILES, The urban mesh of England and Wales, *Transactions of the Institute of British Geographers* no. 11 (1946), 87–101.

For a useful critique of methods of measuring urban centrality see

W. K. D. DAVIES. The ranking of service centres: a critical review, *Transactions of the Institute of British Geographers*, no. 40 (1966), 51–65.

An American example is

J. BRUSH, The hierarchy of central places in southwestern Wisconsin, *Geographical Review* **43** (1953), 380–402.

On the reality of the urban hierarchy see

B. J. L. BERRY and W. L. GARRISON, Functional bases of the central place hierarchy, *Economic Geography* **34** (1958), 145–54.

W. Christaller's earliest work, which has influenced much later writing, is

Die zentralen Orte in Süddeutschland (Jena, 1933). This has been translated into English by C. BASKIN as *The Central Places of Southern Germany* (Englewood Cliffs, 1966).

This, and other work, is discussed in

E. ULLMAN, A theory of location for cities, *American Journal of Sociology* **46** (1941), 853–64.

August Lösch's analysis of location theory has been translated into English as

The Economics of Location (New Haven, 1954).

The rank–size rule is advanced in

G. K. ZIPF, *Human Behaviour and the Principle of Least Effort* (Cambridge, 1949).

A general study of the geometry behind geography is

W. BUNGE, *Theoretical Geography* (Lund, 1962).

The best general study of the rôle of locational analysis not only in urban geography, but also in other branches of the subject is

P. HAGGETT, *Locational Analysis in Human Geography* (London, 1965).

The application of central place and other ideas to a specialist branch of urban geography is

P. SCOTT, *Geography and Retailing* (London, 1970).

CHAPTER 6

THE CITY CENTRE

THE centre of a modern city exhibits special features of land use and possesses distinctive functions which make this the best known of the various regions found within urban areas. Not only has the city centre evoked most interest among those scholars who have studied the functioning of urban areas, but it is also the district with which both casual visitors and permanent residents are familiar. Perhaps because of this variety of interest a range of terms has been applied to the city centre, not all of them meaning exactly the same thing.

Colloquially, for example, the centre is often known as "downtown", a description which is usually applied to that part of the centre which is occupied by entertainment facilities and by the largest department stores. In geographical literature, particularly in America, the city centre is commonly called the *Central Business District*. This has been defined as the area of a city where the retailing of goods and services and the performance of various office activities for private profit are completely dominant. These uses are increasingly found in other parts of cities, but not at the same level of intensity and not occupying the extensive compact area found at the centre. In British planning literature the term *Central Area* is more often used. This is a zone defined on an *ad hoc* basis by the planning agencies of individual cities to delimit an area where certain specific types of planning problem are found (Fig. 32).

Clearly the terms "Central Area" and "Central Business District" refer to two distinct concepts. Central Areas, as usually defined, include streets where central business functions are found, but they also contain residual industrial and residential zones. Taken together these areas often form the historical core of a city, which, in effect, represents its total urban area in the pre-railway age. The areas devoted to residence and industry are intermixed with land uses more typical of the city centre, and are found either at the edge of the Central Area or in the interstices between the main shopping streets. As a result, a distinction

111

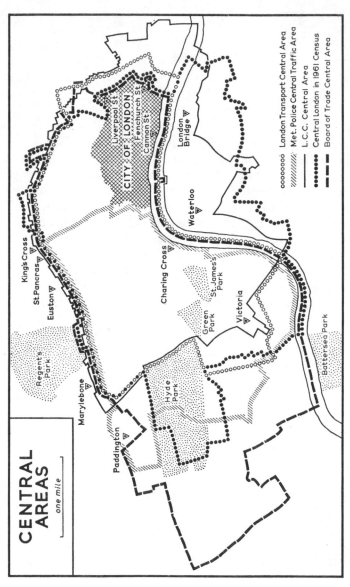

Fig. 32. Central area of London, as defined for various statistical and planning purposes. (*Source*: Based on *Royal Commission on Local Government in Greater London, 1957–60*, map 12.)

between the Central Area and the Central Business District is easier to make in theory than in practice.

Nor is the Central Business District without its ambiguities. The use of land for public administration, which may be found in a city centre for very good reasons, is expressly excluded from many definitions of the Central Business District. So too are such features as churches and educational establishments, although such uses are commonly located in city centres and to exclude them often makes the delimitation of a compact Central Business District almost impossible. As a result, no purist stance will be adopted here: an attempt will be made to describe city centres as they are, rather than as what they should be like in theory.

Accessibility as a Characteristic Feature

Accessibility is the dominant factor influencing the character of the city centre. This is the section of the city which can be most easily reached from the rest of the built-up area. It is also the part most generally accessible to those people who live within a city's sphere of influence, especially if they travel by public transport. In a very large city (particularly if it is the most important urban settlement in a state) its probable position at the focus of the national communications network will also make its city centre accessible to the whole nation, or at least to a very substantial part of it. It is no accident that the central business districts of large cities are frequently located within a ring of railway terminals. A large metropolis is also likely to be at the centre of international routes. Air passengers, for example, although they may land at suburban airports, are brought by bus or some other means of rapid transit to a terminal in the city centre.

This location at the effective centre of a diverse network of communications strongly influences the kind of activities found in the central area. Accessibility from the whole city and its immediate hinterland is particularly important for shops, of which there are a number of types. Most notable are those retail outlets, like department stores and chain shops, which depend on serving the very large number of customers most easily brought together in the city centre. Shops of this kind are found on the principal shopping streets, since they must obtain a site where they can be easily found and attract passing shoppers.

Then there are those highly specialized shops which depend on relatively few scattered customers. Specialist book stores form an example of this kind of enterprise, as do shops which provide for the needs of particular trades and professions. These businesses are less likely to be found on principal shopping streets, since their potential turnover may not be great enough to allow them to pay a very high rent. Alternatively they simply may not require such an expensive site, as their success is likely to depend on personal recommendation rather than on impulse buying. Yet, although they may not be located where land values are at their peak, nevertheless they will be found in the city centre.

There are also specialist shops with a more general appeal, but which are used relatively infrequently by any individual customer. Such

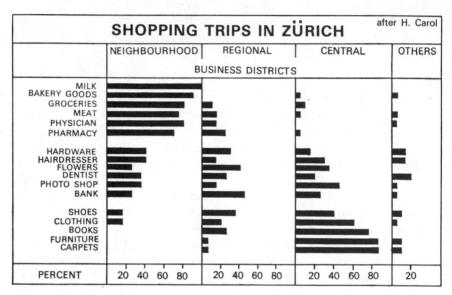

Fig. 33. Shopping trips made by the residents of a Zürich suburb. (*Source:* Carol, in *I.G.U. Symposium in Urban Geography* (1962), p. 564.)

The diagram shows the percentage of shopping trips made by persons residing in Schwamendingen to the local neighbourhood shopping centre, to a regional business district and to the central business district. For the purchase of goods like books, clothing and furniture, the central business district is used by 60 to 80 per cent of the population.

diverse establishments as expensive jewellers, art dealers, exclusive clothing stores and high-class furniture shops all fall into this class. These shops may have a very high turn-over and often have a need to catch the public eye, so that they are more likely to choose a dearer site.

Finally some of the retail outlets in the city centre are not characteristic of this area, but they have been located there to serve customers who have come into the centre for some other reason. Popular restaurants, barbers, tobacconists and newsagents are examples of this kind of shop. As they aim to serve the day-time population of the city centre they tend to be spread through it relatively evenly, although they are likely to be found off the main shopping streets because they are less able to pay the rents of the most desirable sites. Figure 33, for example, illustrates the nature of shopping in central Zürich in comparison with other shopping areas of the city.

Accessibility is also important for many of the offices which are found in a city centre. Some of these require to be located where they can be reached by as many potential clients as possible, in the same way as shops need to tap a reservoir of customers; others must be accessible to their agents who may be working in various parts of a city or its hinterland. A central location also makes it easier for offices to assemble their labour force, which in particular is drawn from middle-class workers, who usually travel daily from scattered localities around the periphery of the built-up area. For the head offices of very important businesses the national and international links of the largest cities are of considerable significance. In the United States, for example, the greatest increase in large offices has been in those cities which possess an international airport. This advantage for the limited number of executives to whom this kind of travel is important appears to be sufficient to control the location of head offices in the centres of these particular cities.

The centres of large cities are also attractive to offices because of the ancillary services which are available there. These include the services of specialist professional firms like lawyers, advertising agents and accountants. In dealing with these professional advisers and with such people as bank managers and the principals of other businesses, the face-to-face contact made possible when all these enterprises are clustered together in a city centre is very important.

This influence is particularly strong for offices which are specially concerned with financial dealings. In this kind of business mutual confidence between those firms which are dealing with each other is important, but is difficult to cultivate except through personal contact. These firms also use the services of such financial institutions as the head offices of banks, stock markets and commodity exchanges; and the need for a location close to these facilities, where again personal contact is involved, leads to the formation of a financial quarter in the Central Area of larger cities.

Figure 34 provides an example of the range and distribution of various activities within the central area of a medium-size European capital city. From this area Sweden in effect is governed; from here too a great part of the country is directed economically. Here, too, is the most important retailing centre in Scandinavia.

The Three-dimensional Quality of City Centres

These various advantages have produced great competition for a site in the city centre among those enterprises which can benefit from such a location. As a result very high land values are found in the centre, a product of this competition. In turn high land values have strongly

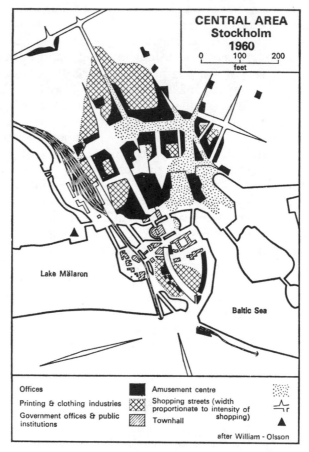

FIG. 34. Some features of central Stockholm, 1960. (*Source*: William-Olsson, *Stockholm: Structure and Development* (1960), p. 92.)

In simplified form this map illustrates the various layers which together give a pronounced structure to central Stockholm. Shopping intensity tapers off away from the centre, but in various areas other activities, like offices and entertainment, are dominant. Between the shopping streets and the office streets the blocks are used for industries, chiefly printing and repair shops of different kinds.

influenced other features found in a city centre. Most notable is the high intensity of land use, which is expressed in the concentration of multi-storied buildings around the area where values are at their peak, a feature which indicates an attempt to erect the maximum floor space which is legally possible on these valuable central sites.

A result of this has been to give city centres a three-dimensional quality, which forms another of their most noticeable characteristics. This feature is most clearly illustrated by American cities, where there are fewer impediments interfering with the role of land values in shaping urban morphology; and it is not surprising that here, at the end of the nineteenth century, the technical advances were made which allowed the erection of very tall buildings.

A fundamental step was taken in Chicago during the 1880's. Iron had been used as a framing material for certain buildings from early in the nineteenth century, but in 1885 a Chicago architect designed an office block in which the walls had no bearing function at all, but were held up by a framework of iron girders, which carried the full weight of the building. The idea was generally adopted and in 1900 steel was substituted for iron in the frame. The advantages of this new system were great. The weight of buildings in relation to their bulk was greatly reduced, thus diminishing the problem of providing suitable foundations. Not only were tall buildings made technically possible, but they also became economically more worth while. The new method of construction brought economy in building materials, together with greater speed and efficiency in erection. Particularly important, valuable floor space on the lower floors was not wasted in accommodating the immensely thick load-bearing walls which had previously been necessary.

Other necessary technical advances were made about the same time. Without the perfection of a safe and fast passenger lift tall buildings could not have functioned efficiently. The development of such an invention was originally stimulated by the demands of the mine and the factory, and as early as 1851 the first really safe elevator had been demonstrated in New York. By 1890 a much-improved version was available for use in the early American skyscrapers. Improvements were also made in the techniques for fire-proofing buildings; and this was an essential step, since fire in very tall buildings was potentially a much greater hazard than in structures of conventional height.

A product of these developments has been the distinctive appearance given to the centres of American cities, with tall and bulky buildings ranged along the straight streets of the grid-iron plan. Tall buildings have also created a distinctive environment for the activities carried on in them, which has been partly diffused to other cities as this style of construction has been adopted, sometimes reluctantly. The most important feature of this environment has been the concentration of employment into a relatively small area, which has had its greatest impact on the nature of transport.

As a result, the passenger lift has now become a vital link in the transport network of any large American city. In New York, for example, there are over 30,000 passenger lifts, which every day carry passengers a total of 125,000 miles. Tall buildings have also had an important effect on horizontal transportation. There is not even space on the sidewalks for one-third of the people who work in the centre of most large American cities, and such overloading makes the streets much less efficient for their task of carrying traffic.

Outside North America, where tall buildings are a newer addition to the urban scene, the concentration of employment in city centres is still taking place. In central London, for example, some 15,000 extra jobs have been created every year during the last decade, producing a related (and unprofitable) increase in the peak loads which have to be carried by commuter services. This increase in employment has largely been the result of the rebuilding and redevelopment of offices, often in structures which rise higher than has previously been the practice in central London.

Important, too, is the struggle for light and air which is caused by building high. Early skyscrapers interfered intolerably with the daylight of their neighbours and resulted in the American set-back regulations, which improved matters in the 1930's. In post-war Britain the growth of similar problems has been dealt with by the production of more flexible day-lighting codes. These ensure that proposed buildings will themselves receive an adequate amount of daylight and will not unduly reduce the light received by neighbouring buildings. These codes are particularly important in dealing with areas of very intensive development in city centres.

Yet the environment created by tall buildings in city centres has strong advantages as well as disadvantages. By permitting many different enterprises to group together on a relatively small area of land, it has proved particularly suitable for creating the close relationships between groups of businessmen which have already been discussed. Similarly, the rise of great commercial organizations during the late nineteenth and twentieth centuries has led to the building of centrally located head offices, which profit from the concentration of their extensive activities in a large building on a compact site. A simpler example of these functional advantages is provided by the large hotel. Such an enterprise appears to function well in a tall building, with a large number of bedrooms, many providing a good view from their windows, being concentrated vertically over the administrative and service operations on the lower floors.

Not that the same use is always made of every floor in a central building. Retail shops, which require immediate access from the street if they are to be successful, must pay the higher rents necessary to obtain ground floor premises. Other users, who do not need sites which will attract passing trade but still require a central location, are often found on upper floors where rents are lower. Examples of this kind of enterprise are the offices of solicitors and wholesale suppliers. Outside the core of the city centre, non-central uses like the storage of goods and certain kinds of manufacturing are also found on upper floors. These businesses, although not central business district users in the strict sense, still require close proximity to the centre as they are often closely linked to genuine central activities. High-class clothing manufacturers, jobbing printers, furriers and small jewellery manufacturers are examples of the typical enterprises found in this location.

Vertical variations in rents, which are closely associated with these different uses, are analogous to the same variations which occur on a horizontal traverse away from the area of peak land values. But the comparison is not quite identical. In tall modern buildings, located on the right spot, the top floors may be made to yield higher rents than some of the lower levels, since a high location has particular appeal for exclusive residential use, for the executive suites of businessmen and, sometimes, for large expensive restaurants.

The Absence of Residential Population

A further characteristic of city centres has been the decline in their residential population which has accompanied the increased concentration of commercial activities within them. The number of people living in the historic cores of Western cities has been falling steadily since the middle of the nineteenth century, the precise date depending on the individual circumstances of a particular settlement. In London, for example, population in the central boroughs has been falling since about 1861, so that today the Central Area (as defined by the Registrar-General) contains little more than 270,000 people, a remarkably low figure for an urban area of nearly 12 square miles (Fig. 35).

This area, however, includes considerable amounts of residential property and the actual reduction of population in the true Central Business District has been much more remarkable. In the City of London, which is essentially the financial quarter of London, there was little change in total population between 1801 and 1851. The first decline in numbers, from 128,000 to 112,000, occurred between 1851 and 1861. During the next decade the fall was much sharper, with a loss of nearly 40,000 people. A steady reduction has continued since then, so that by 1921 the population of the City was just over 13,000; and in 1961 it contained less than 5000 residents.

This outward movement of population from city centres has been made possible by improved methods of transport within cities. In the City of London, for example, the considerable decline in population between 1861 and 1871 was associated with the building of four new railway terminals within the boundaries of the City and by a general upsurge of interest among railway companies in the development of suburban passenger traffic. But the demand to move out was greatly stimulated by the rise in land values as non-residential users of land struggled to obtain central sites during the unprecedented urban expansion in the second half of the nineteenth century. Hence residential buildings were bought up for redevelopment, often before their structures had become unsound, and they were replaced by other uses,

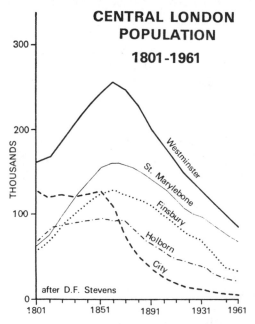

FIG. 35. Population change in the central boroughs of London, 1801–1961. (*Source*: Stevens, in Coppock and Prince (eds.), *Greater London* (1964), p. 173.)

particularly retail shops and offices. Such enterprises were better able to pay for central sites, which were rising rapidly in value as improved means of transport increased the accessibility of city centres and their desirability for these developing uses.

Today the use of land for residential purposes has survived only around the fringes of city centres. Sometimes it consists of residual dwellings which have not yet been rebuilt for some reason or another. Sometimes slums have been replaced by flats, which have been subsidized by a local authority or by some other agency. Sometimes, particularly in the largest cities, residential land use takes the form of luxury dwellings, occupied by those who are rich enough to avoid the journey to work in this way or who desire the social attractions of living near the entertainment and cultural facilities found at the city centre. Yet even in these special cases the use of land for residence is not found where land values are at their peak.

This redistribution of population has encouraged some geographers to describe the centre as the "dead heart" of the city, but that is perhaps too graphic a description, since far more noticeable than the absence of night-time population is the intense concentration of people found during the working day. This concentration poses severe traffic problems, but the resulting congestion is too often interpreted as an unmitigated disaster. In the last resort, congestion is the result of the attraction of the centre for potential customers and for certain kinds of employment which operates in spite of the difficulties involved. This is not to deny that traffic problems in the centre of larger cities are grave and are becoming worse. There are signs that the increasing difficulty of travel is reducing the attraction of some city centres, since congestion is tending to cancel out the inherent accessibility, which is their *raison d'être*.

Certainly the increased use of the motor-car has raised new difficulties. In comparison with other means of urban transportation, like the bus or the underground train, the car carries few people in relation to the amount of space it uses, hence making congestion more severe even with the same number of people travelling. Most cars brought into city centres by daily commuters are unused for much of the day, so there is also the problem of providing unproductive parking space in an area of very high land values. This problem has reached a peak in North American cities, where, in an era of widespread motor-car ownership and in the context of American society, major pieces of traffic engineering have had to be undertaken to maintain the accessibility of city centres for both employees and customers.

In most very large cities, however, the majority of commuters to the city centre still travel by public transport. In these larger cities, too, the contribution of railways to carrying commuters is enhanced, since longer journeys are involved and the problems of driving and parking are at their worst. In the Central Area of London, for example, 91 per cent of people who travel to work use public transport, and of these 83 per cent use underground or main-line railways. Yet public transport services also find difficulties in the central area of cities. Buses are less efficient than they might be because of the general congestion on the roads; and passenger traffic on the railways has been concentrated more and more into a few peak hours, as the private motor-car has increasingly provided transport for leisure activities. As a result excessive amounts of valuable capital equipment have to be kept in reserve to meet peak demand, and labour costs tend to become proportionally higher since efficient use cannot be made of staff throughout the day.

Manufacturing in the Central Business District

Like residential population, manufacturing industry is not normally important in city centres, but certain kinds of manufacturing tend to cluster in and around the centres of large cities. Sometimes these industries are mere relics of past concentrations which are being forced out of the centre by high land values and by the expansion of genuine central business uses. Sometimes specialized areas of manufacturing are still actively flourishing, but are located around the fringes of the city centre, outside the zone of highest land values. Manufacturing in cities will be examined in greater detail in another chapter,* but there is a final type of central manufacturing which it is more appropriate to deal with here. A few specialized manufacturers find it necessary to locate at least some of their processes in the Central Business District proper, the clearest example being the publication of books, periodicals and newspapers.

In book publication the actual printing and binding are now often quite separate from the rest of the business, sometimes undertaken by completely independent firms and often carried on in other settlements many miles away; but editorial work is characteristically an activity of the centre of a metropolis. It can be argued that such a location is not essential for this job, since in the more leisurely world of book publishing contact can be maintained with scattered authors simply by post. Such a view possibly underestimates the need for face-to-face personal contact between publisher and author. In any case, given the relatively small firms in publishing, it is difficult to separate editorial work from other vital activities like the distribution of books and the manipulation of publicity. Thus the attraction of the central business district for the bulk of a publisher's work controls the location of his premises, particularly as administration and distribution play such important parts in this industry.

* See Chapter 8.

In magazine publishing, with a new issue being printed every month or every week, speed in production increases in importance. Editorial processes are much more important in the production of the finished magazine, but in this case immediate access to authors, illustrators, photographers, fashion agencies and similar institutions is an over-riding concern. As a result editorial offices must be easily accessible in the centre of a very large city where other related firms are located. Increasingly these offices are found in metropolitan centres as magazines more and more cater for a national market: in Britain they are almost all located in London and in the U.S.A. most are found in New York. With frequent publication there is also need for a closer contact between editorial office and printer than is found in book production. Periodical printing, however, with its considerable demands for space is moving out of city centres and is commonly undertaken in large suburban works, where bulky deliveries of paper and the dispatch of the finished magazine can be organized more easily, without completely destroying the advantage of rapid and close contact between editor and printer.

The publication of daily newspapers represents a manufacturing industry which for a variety of reasons is even more closely bound to a location in city centres and which is found in a much greater number of cities than other forms of publishing. It is in the centre of cities that news tends to be made and can be collected, often on the basis of personal contacts. Here, too, relationships can be built up with advertising agents, who now provide a large proportion of newspaper revenue. As well as the editorial work, the actual printing of newspapers is carried out in city centres, in spite of the demands on valuable space made by modern printing presses. Here speed of production is vital, and hence it is virtually impossible to separate the printing presses from the editorial department.

Speed of dispatch is also essential. Morning newspapers must be widely distributed during the previous night, since they must be available for early morning deliveries or to be picked up by purchasers on their way to work. In England and Wales, where the printing of morning newspapers is increasingly becoming the monopoly of presses in Manchester and London, deliveries from these two centres have to be made to destinations far outside their immediate hinterlands. In many other countries morning newspapers do not dominate the national market in the way that they do in Britain, but at least papers have to be distributed throughout a city's zone of influence as well as its built-up area. Hence morning newspaper offices require easy access to main-line railway terminals, and this is a further influence encouraging their location in city centres.

Railway stations possibly do not have the same attraction for evening newspaper offices, since these papers are distributed less widely; but the city centre exercises just as great a pull on their location. In many cities a large proportion of sales of evening papers is made in the city centre to workers on their way home. The remainder are often sold within a city's built-up area; and although these papers tend to be distributed to shops and vendors by road rather than by rail, the appeal of a central location remains just as strong.

Internal Specialization within the City Centre

In spite of these various distinctive qualities the city centre is not a homogeneous urban region. Indeed, it might be argued that one of its distinctive features is the degree of internal specialization which is to be found within the central areas of large cities. This specialization exists at a number of scales. In large city centres whole areas may be given a distinctive character by the particular "mix" of enterprises which are found within them. At a more detailed level individual streets may be distinguished by particular kinds of uses. Finally there is even more subtle specialization with, for example, particular types of shops being found in distinctive locations on a shopping street.

Large-scale specialization is a notable feature of the centre of London. Indeed, here it is perhaps better developed than might be normally expected, partly because of its large size, partly owing to the range of specialized functions which the Metropolis fulfils, and partly because of an historical accident. The historical accident was the dual nuclei from which London grew. Medieval London, located on a river terrace close to the oldest part of the port of London, developed into "The City", the financial centre for Britain and beyond. Farther upstream, on another remnant of river terrace, the Crown became the developer of Westminster; and in this area were located the Houses of Parliament and the most important administrative offices of the State. In between these areas lies the "West End", the principal shopping and entertainment centre for south-east England.

The role of historical accident, although an obvious factor in London, should not be pressed too far in explaining specialization within its central area. In New York, for example, a similar contrast exists between the financial quarter of Lower Manhattan and the principal shopping and entertainment area farther north. Yet at least it can be said that every city centre is unique in some respects because of quirks of history. In New York the absence of a distinct area dominated by the legislative and administrative offices of the Federal government is the result of the historical accident which produced a separate Federal capital in Washington.

Broadly speaking, however, the presence of sub-regions within the city centre is the result of its functioning. Various economic and functional links bind together the land uses which characterize these various specialized areas. The links found in the financial quarters of great cities have already been commented upon, but similar ties exist in other specialized areas. Shopping areas, for example, profit from the presence of a large number of retail outlets in a small area, since this concentration is a strong force in attracting potential purchasers to this part of the city centre. Theatres, first-run cinemas and other forms of entertainment profit from each other's presence, since this draws the attention of patrons to the range of shows which are currently running, and the overflow from one place of entertainment to another helps to maintain full houses. Similarly, in capital cities the presence of the legislature and various government administrative offices in the same district adds to the efficiency of their functioning.

Even in smaller city centres the same tendency to form sub-regions also exists. D. R. Diamond, for example, has shown that there are three types of specialized area in the central business district of Glasgow, dominated respectively by offices, wholesaling, and retail shopping; and again these sub-regions reflect the operation of both chance and current economic factors (Fig. 36). In central Glasgow, for instance, retail shopping occupies two distinct areas of approximately equal size and intensity of use. The location of retailing here, as in every other city, owes much to the transportation network and, in this particular case at least, to the distribution of bus terminals. The presence of two central shopping areas, however, is the product of the precise manner in which Glasgow developed and is the result of local historical and physical influences, which led to the growth of two major traffic nodes.

The specialized siting of particular activities is apparent at an even more detailed level. Central furniture stores, for example, tend to cluster together, since potential purchasers are attracted by the possibility of making an easy comparison of what different shops have to offer. Or, again, branches of banks appear to favour a corner site for reasons which are not altogether clear, although local accessibility to neighbouring businesses is presumably important. Something of a mystery is also provided by the clustering of newspaper offices in highly localized parts of city centres, which in London has made the Press synonymous with the name of Fleet Street. Since the advent of telecommunications there can have been little real advantage in this close grouping, although at an earlier period proximity to other newspaper offices must have been more important. There are signs, in London at least, that this concentration is becoming less clearly marked and thus it probably represents a survival of past conditions.

The tendency towards specialization is strongest in those parts of a city centre which possess the highest land values. If the cost of a site is very high, the efficiency of its location for a particular use takes on special significance, since the maximum advantage must be derived from a site if it is to be profitable. As a result relatively small differences between individual sites or particular parts of the city centre are emphasized. Towards the fringes of the centre, however, where land values are

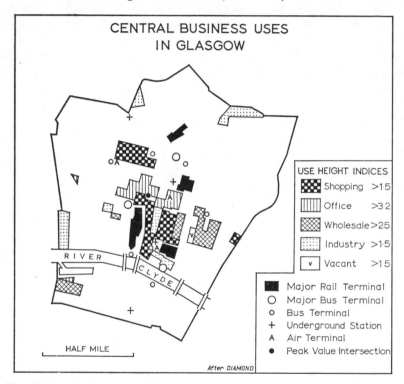

Fig. 36. Specialized areas in central Glasgow. (*Source*: Diamond, in *I.G.U. Symposium in Urban Geography* (1962), p. 530.)

The use/height index measures the ratio between the area devoted to a particular land use in a block of buildings and the ground floor area of the block. In Glasgow the peak values for different types of land use varied considerably and, when plotted, specialized areas were delimited.

lower, uses tend to be less segregated. In Glasgow, for example, Diamond has observed a three-fold division of the central area. First there is the area with specialized uses, which forms a core. Around this is a zone where the use of land is still very intense, but uses are less segregated and are best described by the general term "commercial". Finally there is a boundary zone where uses characteristic of the city centre are intermixed with non-central uses.

In fact, the recognition of core areas has been given considerable attention in geographical studies of city centres. These studies have been inspired by the observation that in the most accessible part of city centres nearly all the available floor space is devoted to central business uses, and that these uses occupy a greater number of floors than elsewhere in the centre. To take one example, D. H. Davies has shown that in Capetown there is a clearly defined core area where an average of at least four floors in every city block and at least 80 per cent of the total available floor space are devoted to central business uses. This core area is notable for the density of its traffic and for the high value of its land. Just for this latter reason, however, there is more chance of finding detailed specialization within it.

For that matter, even in the so-called "hard core" area there are failings in a definition based purely on the use of land for private profit. There can be few cities with any length of history which do not have considerable areas devoted to activities which are not central business uses in the strict sense of the term. In London, for example, the area of highest commercial land values is in a zone around the Bank of England, but this institution itself is not operating for private profit. Close by, the great mass of St. Paul's Cathedral also provides an important anomaly, which affects not only the area on which it actually stands, but also, because of aesthetic considerations, limits the height and layout of the surrounding commercial buildings. More extensive areas where similar distortions are found include the government administrative quarter in Westminster and the growing university area in Bloomsbury. Hence the form of the centre of nearly every city is not merely a matter of land economics, although this remains a factor of the utmost importance.

Selected Reading

Methods of delimiting the boundaries of central business districts are discussed in
R. E. MURPHY and J. E. VANCE Jr., Delimiting the CBD, *Economic Geography* **30** (1954), 189–222.

The economic background to the location of shops in the city centre is discussed in
R. U. RATCLIFF, *Urban Land Economics* (New York, 1949), pp. 123–38.

On tall buildings in the city see
J. H. JOHNSON, The geography of the skyscraper, *Journal of Geography* **55** (1956), 349–63;

J. GOTTMANN, Why the skyscraper?, *Geographical Review* **56** (1966), 190–212.

A study of many of the aspects of central London is

D. F. STEVENS, The Central Area, in J. T. Coppock and H. C. Prince (eds.), *Greater London* (London, 1964), pp. 167–201.

An analysis of the economic background to the functioning of the financial quarter is

J. H. DUNNING, The City of London: a case study in urban economics, *Town Planning Review* **40** (1969), 207–32.

The publication of newspapers and periodicals in central New York City is described in

W. E. GUSTAFSON, Printing and publishing, in M. Hall (ed.), *Made in New York: Case Studies in Metropolitan Manufacturing* (Cambridge, Mass., 1959), pp. 135–239.

An interesting study of the internal differentiation of the central area of a particular city is

D. R. DIAMOND, The central business district of Glasgow, in K. Norborg (ed.), *Proceedings of the I.G.U. Symposium in Urban Geography, Lund 1960* (Lund, 1962), pp. 525–34.

On this same topic see also

H. CARTER and G. ROWLEY, The morphology of the central business district of Cardiff, *Transactions of the Institute of British Geographers* no. 38 (June 1966), 119–34.

An example of an attempt to find a "core" within the centre of a particular city is

D. H. DAVIES, The hard core of Cape Town's central business district: an attempt at delimitation, *Economic Geography* **36** (1960), 53–69.

See also

D. H. DAVIES, *Land Use in Central Capetown: a study in urban geography* (Capetown, 1965).

The problems of commuting by rail to the central area of London are examined in

H. P. WHITE, London's rail terminals and their suburban traffic: a geographic appraisal of the commuter problem, *Geographical Review* **54** (1964), 347–65.

And a sample study of road traffic associated with a group of buildings in the centre of Manchester is found in

I. BOILEAU, Traffic and land use, *Town Planning Review* **29** (1958), 27–42.

Features of the outer limits of the central business district are summarized in

R. E. PRESTON, Transition zone structure: the three sector hypothesis, *Town Planning Review* **39** (1968), 235–50.

See also parallel articles by

R. E. PRESTON, in *Economic Geography* **42** (1966), 237–44, and (with D. W. Griffin) in *Annals of the Association of American Geographers* **56** (1966), 339–50.

CHAPTER 7

RESIDENTIAL SUBURBS

AN OUTSTANDING feature of most large modern cities is the growth around them of extensive residential suburbs. This expansion is partly a result of the increasing populations of those cities whose dynamic economies allow them to attract migrants and to retain the natural increase of their own populations. The impact of population growth is increased by the tendency in many affluent societies for family units to become smaller and more independent. Hence, even if urban population totals are stable, more dwelling units are required to house the same number of people.

A further element in suburban expansion is the growing wish of people to live at lower densities. In part this desire reflects a current architectural fashion;* but it is also encouraged by more positive reasons than mere whim. For one thing, low-density dwellings have many functional advantages for family living, particularly when a family contains young children. For another, cheapness of construction is important since, square foot for square foot, high-density housing is more expensive to build than low-density; and, although more land is required for housing of this kind, normally it is available more cheaply in suburban locations. Whatever the causes, the detached or, at least, the semi-detached house has become the ultimate goal of more and more people.

Such a desire would have had little influence on the urban landscape if it had not been accompanied by the necessary ability to convert it from dream to reality. But the prosperity of industrialized (and urbanized) countries is a recurrent theme in the modern world and the rewards of affluence are being increasingly diffused among all the social classes of these urban communities. As a result, a real and growing demand has been created for low-density housing, which has at least been partially satisfied by countless acres of suburban building, often architecturally undistinguished.

* See Chapter 2, p. 36

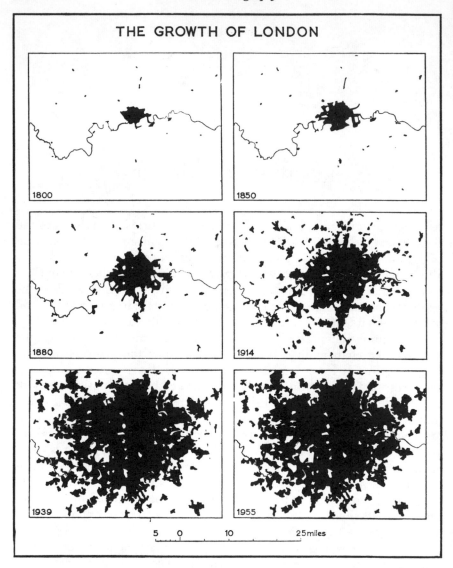

THE GROWTH OF LONDON

1800

1850

1880

1914

1939

1955

5   0   10   25 miles

Fig. 37. The growth of London.

In the pre-railway era the built-up area of London remained compact. Expansion in the second half of the nineteenth century was more rapid, with tram and steam-railway services encouraging longer journeys to work. In the twentieth century, the extension of the underground to outer London, the electrification of surface railways, the growing importance of travel by bus and motor-car, and the development of suburban industry all led to an unprecedented expansion of the built-up area.

The United States provides the classic case of a nation in which the extent of suburbs has exploded during the twentieth century. Although statistics are a notoriously unreliable indicator of detailed changes around the fringes of cities, the official census returns record some 30 million suburban dwellers in the U.S.A. for 1950, a figure which gives some hint of the relative importance of this growth. Not only does this represent a substantial proportion of a total population of 150 millions, but the rate of change is also increasing its momentum. Between 1947 and 1955, for example, 9 million people in the U.S.A. moved into suburban homes.

Although not always so dramatic, the history of suburban growth around all Western cities (or indeed around cities of other cultures which have been adopting Westernized economies) is basically similar. In detail, however, the generic resemblance varies from place to place, as a result of differences in the timing of suburban growth and in the speed of building, related in turn to local technological and economic developments. The recent history of suburban growth in Britain and the United States illustrates this point.

Suburban Growth in Britain and the United States between the Wars

In the United States suburban developments in the late nineteenth century were largely confined to narrow belts near those railways which provided suitable services to commuters, or along roads served by trams. The First World War may be taken as the end of this era, since in the 1920's a vast increase in suburban building occurred, with very large housing estates being a dominant feature. Here an important factor was the return from the war of ex-service men, setting up home for the first time and creating a larger demand for new and relatively cheap homes than had ever been experienced before. Equally important, and in the long run more significant, was the impact of increased motor-car ownership. Even by 1915 there were $2\frac{1}{2}$ million cars in the U.S.A., but by 1920 that number had grown to 9 million. In the next ten years the number of cars again nearly trebled, reaching $26\frac{1}{2}$ million by 1930. As a result more people were able to travel longer distances to work and the increased flexibility of travel associated with motor-cars opened up new tracts of land for residential development. These lay between main roads or around the rapidly expanding outer fringes of cities; and detached from the continuous built-up areas of large cities, smaller towns also became dominated by commuters.

Britain, too, experienced the same greatly increased demand for houses, but during the early 1920's suburban expansion was less drama-tic. Partly this was because the recovery of the British building industry from wartime conditions appears to have been slower, and the industry was less geared to the mass production of houses. In Britain, too, the motor-bus was more important as a new means of urban transport. Although more flexible than the tram, its impact in opening up new areas for urban development was not as great as that of the private car.

During the 1930's there was again a contrast between the two coun-tries. In the United States the Depression considerably slowed down the rate of suburban expansion. Taken as a whole, this was a period when the fringes of many cities grew more modestly and the gaps left during the previous era of rapid development were filled in. In the early 1930's there was almost a halt to new building in many parts of the U.S.A. In the later 1930's, however, a considerable number of more modest houses or suburban apartment houses were constructed; and it was in this period that the extension of the built-up areas of many cities occurred, to be checked by the Second World War. In all, between 1930 and 1945 the growth of suburban population just about reflected the rate of growth in the total population of the United States.

In Britain, on the other hand, there was no comparable check on house-building until 1939; and, paradoxically enough, in some parts of the country the financial results of the Depression positively en-couraged suburban building. The impact of the Depression in Britain varied in different parts of the country. The London area and its surroundings were relatively prosperous at this time, for here a large share of the growing sectors of the national economy were concen-trated. Hence it is not surprising that over one-third of the houses erected by private builders in England and Wales between 1930 and 1939 were located in the Home Counties.

The rise in the production of houses in Britain was the result of a number of factors (Fig. 38). One of these was the strength of the building society movement. During this period of economic uncertainty building societies were popular outlets for investment and, in turn, were anxious to lend money to house purchasers. Many societies made special arrangements with builders so that only very small deposits were required from prospective purchasers; after 1932 interest rates fell; and a reduction in the price of building materials also reduced the actual costs of construction.

This situation also encouraged a change in the form of new housing developments. The building societies' arrangements to reduce deposits favoured the larger building firms because of their superior credit-worthiness; and large builders were more likely to build big housing estates. This gave the larger firms a further advantage, since labour could be saved in the construction of extensive rather than small groups of houses; and there were also economies to be made through the bulk

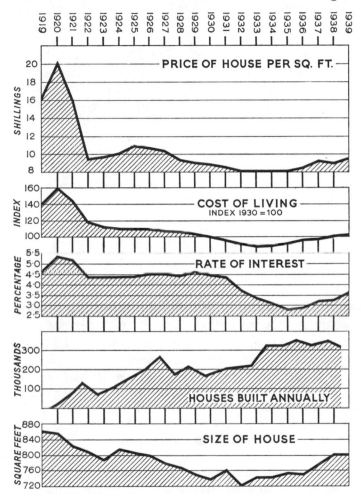

FIG. 38. Factors influencing house-building in England and Wales, 1919–39. (*Source*: Based on data in Ministry of Health, *The Cost of House-Building: First Report of the Committee of Inquiry* (1948), p. 60.)

purchase of materials and the use of standardized parts. As a result, the typical house of the 1930's more commonly formed part of a large estate, a type of development which reflected the growth of large building companies and the need to streamline production for a highly competitive market. There was also a slight change in the average size of houses being built. After the impediment of finding a large deposit had been reduced, the range of people who were able to move into new, privately owned houses was broadened; but the annual outgoings which they could afford was more restricted, so that the average house of this period tended to be smaller, reflecting the lower income of many purchasers.

In many areas away from south-east England, where the Depression had more impact, a much greater proportion of houses were built by local government authorities, rather than by speculative builders. The morphology of the resulting developments, however, was not greatly different, since terrace and semi-detached houses, all with two storeys, with gardens and built at relatively low densities, were characteristic of these council estates. Socially, they were working-class rather than lower-middle-class developments; but demographically the distinction was less clear, as these council estates were also dominated by young married couples and their children.

Developments since the Second World War

The Second World War brought a break in house-building both in the United States and in Britain, and since 1945 it has again been possible to distinguish slight differences in the form of residential suburbs in the two countries. In Britain, reflecting the more limited space available for urban development and the differing political climate of the two countries, planning control has been more active in preventing the formless spread of residential building. This control has applied throughout Great Britain since 1947, although it has been most rigorously applied around London. Here, a "Green Belt" was delimited on the various county development plans approved by the central government between 1954 and 1958, and this belt was expressly designed to check the outward expansion of the continuous built-up area of the metropolis (Fig. 39). Taken as a whole, land use planning in Britain has tidied up the form of residential expansion and made it more compact. It has also checked to some extent the rise in the number of urban workers who live in rural areas, and prevented building on some of the more attractive and agriculturally valuable areas near cities.

In the United States car ownership has continued to expand more rapidly, building was less restricted by shortages in the years immediately after the war, and there have been fewer fears of agricultural land being swamped by building. As a result, the growth of suburbs here has been so dramatic since the Second World War that the expression "the flight to the suburbs" has been frequently used by writers on American cities, sometimes with the implication that a new pattern in urban growth had been established. In fact, this is not strictly true: the statistics quoted often show no more than the discrepancy

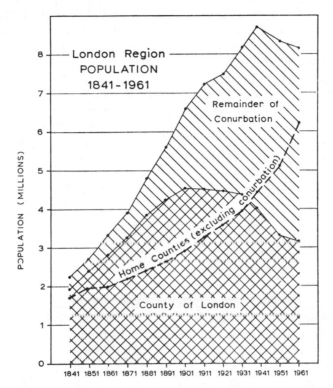

Fig. 39. Population growth in and around London, 1841–1961. (*Source:* Based on statistics in Coppock and Prince (eds.), *Greater London* (1964), p. 34.)

This graph serves as an example of the expansion of population in the outer suburbs of a British city in the twentieth century. These figures indicate the growing discrepancy between the limits of a city as legally defined and its actual limits as a functioning unit of settlement. In recent decades the actual expansion of London has been taking place, not in its continuous built-up area, but in towns and villages in the surrounding counties.

between the limits of individual cities as legally defined and the limits of actual cities as functioning units of settlement, which frequently include unincorporated settlements on the urban fringe.

Nevertheless, there are a number of new elements which have introduced a faster pace of suburban development. Just before the First

World War industry was beginning to discover the advantages of a sub-urban location, and this trend was elaborated between the wars.* The growth of employment in the outer ring of cities encouraged suburban residential expansion between the wars and this same process continued with undiminished force after the Second World War. In addition, an increased amount of the more routine forms of office employment has been moving to the suburbs, partly following the female labour force, and partly driven out by rising land values and increased congestion in city centres. This trend is found in many parts of the Western world; but a further stimulus to suburban growth in the post-war period has been more restricted to the United States, although it is very likely that it will spread elsewhere in due course. This is the construction of sub-urban regional shopping centres, which are an expression of the great rise in the number of privately owned cars, of the growing purchasing power of American households, and of the physical expansion of larger cities.

A second element creating a new situation around American cities in particular is the shifting balance between the growth of urban popula-tion and the rate at which new buildings are being constructed. The demand for housing after 1945 was inflated by the halt in building during the war and by the impact of rising marriage rates in the 1940's, with the result that the economics of mass production have been further applied to the building of large housing estates. Hence during the post-war period there has been an accelerated redistribution of population from older homes to relatively undeveloped areas around the fringes of cities, where an improved environment for living can be provided more cheaply than by the redevelopment of existing resi-dential areas.

The Rise of Distinctive Residential Areas

Looking beyond these detailed variations occurring from time to time and place to place, two distinctive features stand out in the sub-urban residential areas of modern cities. One of these is the tendency for residential areas to be segregated from other uses of land, with suburban industry being confined to distinct zones and retail distribution being gathered into compact shopping centres. The other outstanding fea-tures of residential suburbs is for continuous areas to be occupied by a single social class. This segregation is clear at two scales. In detail, individual estates or groups of houses are built for single income-groups; and, on a broader scale, whole sectors of towns and cities appear to be dominated by distinct social classes.

* See Chapter 8, pp. 161–5

These features are largely a product of developments in the twentieth century, since many typical nineteenth-century suburbs did not possess the same degree of homogeneity as their modern counterparts. In nineteenth-century middle-class suburbs, for example, there were a substantial number of servants living "below stairs". Local trades-people also worked and lived close by, since they had to be reached on foot or, possibly, by carriage. Although towards the end of the century the provision of street-car services in larger cities allowed more flexible journeys to work and a greater amount of grouping by social class, the pattern created was still more diverse than in a twentieth-century city. Once longer journeys to work became possible some sectors of a city could more easily become distinctive, but superimposed on this broad design was a "weave" of smaller patterns, made up of small groups of distinctive houses and streets rather than large undifferentiated zones of residential buildings.

During the twentieth century a changed situation was created. The number of families who could afford servants declined. The greater flexibility of movement within cities, produced by the continued im-provement of public transport services and the wider diffusion of car ownership, allowed more sorting of social groups and the concentration of different land uses into distinct parts of a city. In many cities zoning ordinances were devised; and although these restrictions did not repre-sent positive planning in a modern sense, they prevented the location of shops and manufacturing plants within residential areas and applied standard housing densities over considerable districts. As a result, large sections of the new twentieth-century suburbs were covered with houses of the same size and on the same site areas. These houses, therefore, were within the same price range and attracted people in the same social class (Figs. 40 and 41).

Whether guided by natural processes or municipal ordinances, the decision on the kind of houses appropriate for different parts of a city was often made by speculative builders, whose assessment reflected the social priorities of the local community. Scenic attractiveness, the avail-ability of good commuter services, the location of the homes of the cur-rent leaders of local society—these and similar features controlled the areas in which the more expensive houses were built and where the better-off members of society came to live. On the other hand, those areas which were flat, uninteresting, inconvenient and close to heavy industry were likely to be occupied by those people who could only afford the cheapest new houses. Various gradations of residential land value and social class existed between these two extremes.

Meanwhile readjustments were also taking place in the older

residential areas built in the nineteenth century. Perhaps least change
was found in those older areas dominated by artisans' houses, whose
inhabitants remained relatively unaltered. These homes were not large
enough to subdivide, but ultimately, as their structures deteriorated,
poorer people might well take them over. Larger middle-class homes
were more susceptible to change. Big enough to be subdivided and built
for that section of the community most aware of changing fashion, these

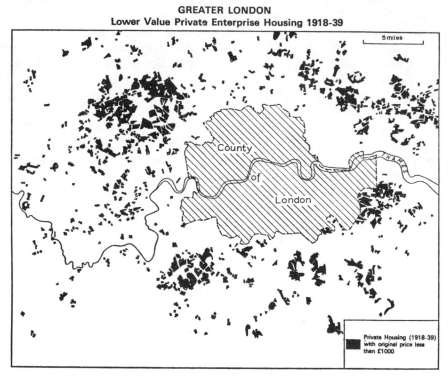

Fig. 40. Greater London: lower value private enterprise housing, 1918–39.
(*Source*: Johnson, in Coppock and Prince (eds.), *Greater London* (1964), p. 147.)

houses were occupied by their original purchasers for a shorter period.
After a number of decades, when they had lost some of their original
social lustre or when repairs were becoming a larger element in their
cost, these houses experienced what might be called "social leap-
frogging", as they were occupied by a series of groups lower in the social
"pecking order". Eventually these older middle-class houses were more
likely to become slums, because their very size made them more suitable
for subdivision.

In some cities, however, a few inner residential areas maintained their status, since for a variety of reasons their inhabitants were not attracted by new houses in the growing twentieth-century suburbs. Some people clung to their more central homes to avoid the ever-lengthening journey to work and to maintain contact with the social and cultural life of the city centre. This tendency was particularly strong if their houses were

GREATER LONDON
Higher Value Private Enterprise Housing 1918-39

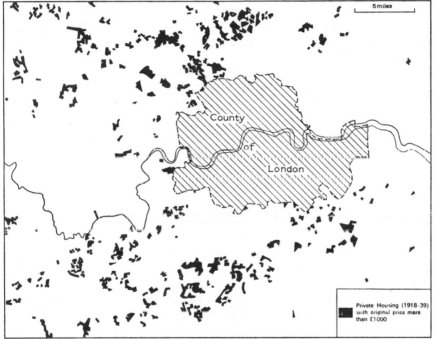

FIG. 41. Greater London: higher value private enterprise housing, 1918–39.
(*Source*: Johnson, in Coppock and Prince (eds.), *Greater London* (1964), p. 148.)

built in the fashionable Georgian style and were located in socially approved districts. Beacon Hill in Boston, for example, maintained itself as a desirable area, in spite of the growing obsolescence of its houses, because a few important people chose to remain there, thus bolstering the social desirability of this district. Indeed, in a number of very large cities the desire to live in certain inner residential areas has actually forced up land values to such an extent that the existing population has been edged out. In London, for example, artisans' houses in parts of

Chelsea and Kensington have been taken over by middle-class residents. Now without servants, they have not been deterred by the smaller size of these houses, but have been attracted by their convenient location and by their proximity to even grander dwellings and neighbours.

With the exception of a few areas of upper-class housing close to the centres of some large cities, the average social status of suburban areas in modern Western cities is higher than that of the inner residential areas. In the non-Western world, particularly in those tropical cities which have been growing dramatically in recent decades, a different situation often exists. Here the many very poor people, who have been attracted by the small cash income which they can obtain from casual employment, often form large communities of squatters around the fringes of the urban areas.

The number of squatters in some of these cities has reached remarkable proportions. In 1959, for example, Delhi was estimated to have 200,000 squatters, forming 13 per cent of its population. In 1961 Djarkarta was said to have 750,000 squatters, which constituted 25 per cent of its population, and in the same year the 100,000 squatters of Kuala Lumpur formed 20 per cent of that city's population. Nor is this phenomenon restricted to Asia. The shanty towns of Latin America are famous (or infamous): these settlements are the *favelas* of Brazil, the *villas de miseria* of Argentine, and the *barrios* of Venezuela. The shanty towns of some African cities—the *bidonvilles* of the former French colonies—are also notorious.

Squatter settlements are generally located around the fringes of the built-up area, where land is available which is not in demand for other urban purposes. Here squatters can occupy sites which are not claimed by their legal owners or which can be obtained on very cheap rents. In a few cases squatters have managed to occupy inner sections of cities, as for example in Manila, where they settled for some time on an area close to the original core of the city, which had been devastated during the Second World War and was therefore open to occupation of this kind.

Although shanty towns are common in areas of rapid urban growth, particularly in climates where flimsy houses provide some protection against the elements, the forces involved in their development are not purely economic. One important social force is the desire among immigrants to live in a society which provides a transition between life in their home villages and that in the city proper. Shanty towns also imply a legal situation in which zoning regulations do not prevent their growth, either because planning control is not well developed or because there is little desire among residents of a higher social status to preserve suburban areas for their exclusive occupation.

Perhaps these suburban communities of squatters can be seen as a transitory phase in the urban geography of the developing countries. Already shanties have been replaced by blocks of flats in such cities as Hong Kong, Manila and Caracas. Such changes, however, are only possible in relatively prosperous cities. Shanty towns are probably more permanent features in those cities which have been swamped by immigrants and, at the same time, are without the resources to remove a *fait accompli*. Although there may be a genuine desire to tear down these areas, which are perhaps socially rootless, which are probably breeding grounds for disease, and which are certainly aesthetically undesirable, the means to do the job properly, without creating even greater hardship for these unfortunate people, are often lacking at present.

Suburban Retail Outlets

The nature of suburban growth around large Western cities has led to a contrast in the distribution and form of shops which serve older and newer residential areas; and the general topic of retail distribution in the suburbs thus requires some more detailed examination. In the late nineteenth century the pattern of shopping was dominated by the central business district, which was at this time in the process of acquiring large stores with massive turn-overs. Other shops were lined along roads served by public transport, especially at accessible junctions on these roads, where in large cities distinct nuclei of shops formed. Finally, individual "corner" shops were scattered about the residential areas of nineteenth-century cities.

These features survived into the twentieth century, but a change of emphasis took place in new developments. Although the amount of business done in city centres did not decline, its rate of increase was much less than in suburban areas, where people were usually more prosperous than the average and were less willing to travel into city centres for their more frequent requirements. These new suburban shops exhibited a number of distinctive features and the pattern of retailing in suburban areas is still actively changing.

These developments have been most dramatic in the United States, which may be taken as an example, but similar tendencies are apparent elsewhere in the Western world. In the new suburbs the services provided by isolated "convenience goods" shops were too restricted for the more prosperous inhabitants of these areas and, in any case, the presence of isolated shops was socially unacceptable in the semi-rural setting of the new houses. As a result the bottom layer of the suburban shopping hierarchy consisted of isolated clusters of shops, designed to serve a neighbourhood with its day-to-day wants (Fig. 42). Today, with the tendency towards larger shopping units, many of these neighbourhood clusters are being replaced by a single supermarket.

Larger groups of shops were found where strips of commercial land use spread along the more convenient arterial roads in the suburbs, and reflected the rising importance of the car in American shopping in the

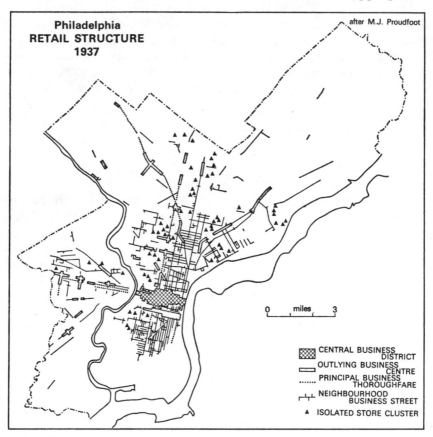

Fig. 42. Retail structure of Philadelphia, 1937. (*Source*: Proudfoot, *Economic Geography* **13** (1937), 426.)

> In a classic study M. J. Proudfoot recognized five types of shopping centre in a typical United States' city in the 1930's. Since then an important new trend has been the growth of planned shopping centres, often located on the urban fringe and owned by a single agency, which controls the architecture of the centre, the types of shops accepted and the provision of parking.

1920's. In the 1930's a new feature was added to these unplanned centres when multiple stores began to pursue the outlying mass market.

Sometimes a single department store was erected on a favourable site and this formed the basis of an unplanned cluster of larger shops. The firm of Sears Roebuck, for example, was particularly active in establishing suburban department stores, aimed at the motorist shopper.

Since the Second World War the colonization of the suburbs by multiple stores has continued at a much-increased rate. Between 1948 and 1954 retail sales in the forty-eight largest Metropolitan Areas of the United States rose by 32 per cent, but the increase in their central business districts was only 1·6 per cent. The suburban expansion of retailing

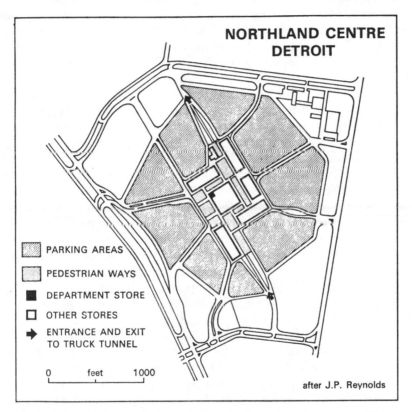

FIG. 43. Northland Centre, Detroit: a suburban shopping centre. (*Source*: Reynolds, *Town Planning Review* **29** (1958), 49.)

implied in these figures often took the form of more formally planned shopping centres of various sizes, but all designed with the motor-car expressly in mind (Fig. 43). These new planned centres differ from earlier groups of shops in that the ownership of their land is retained by the developer, thus ensuring unified control of design. As the developers often receive a share of the profits made by the individual shops, they carefully select the tenants by the profitability of their businesses on this particular type of site.

The largest of the planned centres, which often contain several department stores, are intended to serve a population of over 250,000 each, and hence draw their customers not only from the residential areas immediately around them, but also from a larger sector of the cities in which they are situated. Smaller planned centres repeat the pattern found in these regional centres, in that they are based on relatively large chain stores, providing standardized goods for a mass market. Those centres designed to serve 50,000 to 200,000 people are often built around a smaller department store; those serving a population of 30,000 to 50,000 are centred around a variety store, like those belonging to F. W. Woolworth; and those serving a population of from 7,000 to 15,000 are commonly built around a supermarket.

These centres of themselves make a considerable demand upon space, since one of their basic attractions is the improved parking which they offer. As one large American car in an unattended park uses 330 square feet of space and as some of the larger centres have a capacity for 10,000 parked cars at any one time, merely the provision of car parks on this scale implies the use of large areas of land. Even more important, these centres make suburban life more convenient and more orientated to a society dominated by the motor-car. By lessening the need for visits by housewives to city centres and by stimulating the ownership of more than one car per family, they are encouraging the further development of low-density housing. In some cases these centres have actually pioneered the extension of the built-up areas of cities.

Shopping centres in Britain have not been dominated by the motor-car to the same extent as in America, and (except in a few isolated cases) more stringent planning controls and less general ownership of cars have so far prevented the building of new centres for the motorist shopper outside the built-up areas of existing cities. Nevertheless, cities which acquired extensive areas of suburbs during the twentieth century have also developed their own system of suburban retail outlets, which bears some similarity to the pattern found elsewhere. A comparable hierarchy of suburban shopping centres is most easily seen in Greater London, where Smailes and Hartley, for example, have recognized regional shopping centres, major suburban shopping centres, minor suburban shopping centres and neighbourhood shopping clusters.

A few regional shopping centres command whole sectors of suburban London, possess the range of services found in the central business district of many a large city, and function in much the same way. The major and minor centres vary considerably in size, but in spite of this, the degree of specialization found in all these suburban centres is remarkably similar. Symptomatic of this is the fact that the tributary areas of major and minor suburban centres are not superimposed on one another, although the number of customers within these areas varies considerably. As a result, although all the suburban shopping centres tend to provide the same kind of goods, there are differences in the nature of the largest shops they possess. For example, a small Woolworth's store is commonly the largest shop found in a minor suburban centre; and a large popular clothing store like Marks and Spencer is not found in anything smaller than a major London suburban centre. This contrast, however, has more to do with the maximum size of shopping unit which can survive in a particular location, rather than with the range of goods and services which a centre offers.

The Journey to Work

As with the pattern of retail distribution, the daily journey to work has also taken on a new significance with the expansion of suburbs, which has affected both the number of people involved and the distances over which they travel. The importance for suburban development of the greater flexibility brought by the motor-car has already been stressed and has been particularly important in America and in those smaller cities where traffic congestion is a less dominating force. In very large cities, however, other means of travel have been equally important. In outer London, for instance, suburban growth between the two world wars was greatly encouraged by three related developments: the scatter of suburban railway stations was thickened; train services were improved; and motor-bus services linked the railway stations more effectively with the areas around them.

The fact that rapid transit routes are most obviously seen to link suburbs with city centres masks some features of the modern journey to work. In smaller cities the journey is sometimes dominated by a simple movement into their centres, but more commonly the rise of suburban manufacturing has greatly complicated the picture. Certainly the daily journey into the central business district gives the clearest indication of the interdependence of the various parts of a great city, yet in many suburbs it is less important than local movements, particularly since the growth of suburban shopping centres has also reduced the need for shopping trips to the centre.

In London a surprising number of journeys from the outer fringe of the Metropolis are over a relatively short distance. In 1951, for example, only 39 per cent of journeys to work in the suburbs could be classified as "long" (i.e. farther than an adjoining local authority area) and only just over half of these long journeys (or 20 per cent of the total journeys to work) were to the centre of London. Fifty-seven per cent of workers had short journeys to destinations within the outer ring of the conurbation and only 7 per cent had long daily journeys to other areas within this outer ring. There is evidence that such a pattern is not uncommon in many large cities.

This general picture is complicated by detailed variations, which are often connected with the social class of a residential area. The more exclusively middle-class areas are less likely to offer local employment and a higher proportion of their population is likely to be in professional and administrative jobs, which are more commonly located in the city centre. Certainly this is true of London where, in 1951, more than a quarter of the night-time population of the more consistently middle-class outer suburbs travelled daily to work in the Central Area. At the other extreme, the outer suburbs of west Middlesex stood out most clearly from the rest of the suburban ring, because they had only tenuous daily links with central London, as a result of the large number of local industrial jobs which they possess and their greater proportion of non-professional residents.

Another feature of the journey to work which is sometimes overlooked is its importance in extending effective urban growth away from the actual built-up area of a large city. Even in the nineteenth century small towns and villages were expanded by the provision of train services to some nearby city; but normally this expansion was in the form of compact building, as these commuters lived within walking distance of their local railway stations. In the twentieth century, however, the influence of the journey to work has been greatly extended and changed.

Aided by the growth of industrial employment both around suburban fringes and in satellite towns, the motor-car has allowed greater freedom of movement around large cities, particularly where journeys are not made into the congested central business districts. In those countries where strong planning control is absent a looser form of urban structure has resulted from this changed journey to work, with houses often being built at very low densities on relatively cheap agricultural land, with the most socially desirable areas located on scenically attractive districts, which are frequently wooded and undulating.

Planning control in Britain, in particular the establishment of a Green Belt around London, has encouraged more compact urban development, although before the Second World War there were a number of areas of very low density, exclusive residential building. Post-war restrictions on building in the open countryside, however, have also tended to hide as well as prevent the process by which urban workers have occupied apparently rural areas. For example, R. E. Pahl has shown that in Hertfordshire, on the fringes of London, the percentage increase of population in rural districts between 1951 and 1961 was greater than that in the county as a whole. Often groups of middle-class commuters have been tacked onto the population of villages within the Green Belt or have been attracted by housing developments beyond the Green Belt where restrictions on building have been less stringently enforced.

ENGLAND AND WALES
THE JOURNEY TO WORK

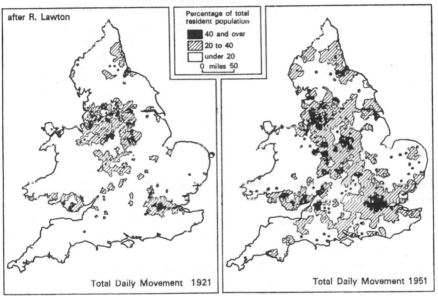

Fig. 44. The journey to work in England and Wales, 1921 and 1951. (*Source:* simplified from Lawton, *Tijdschrift voor Econ. en Soc. Geografie* **54** (1963), 63.)

These maps show the number of people who entered or left local authority areas on a daily journey to work as a percentage of their total resident populations.

A more general indication of this trend is given in R. Lawton's analysis of the journey to work information in the 1921 and 1951 censuses of England and Wales. If the areas contributing daily migrants and those attracting them are taken together as forming part of an urban "system", the amount of daily movement can be seen to have expanded greatly (Fig. 44). In the 1920's many town dwellers travelled quite considerable distances to work, but rural areas were often relatively self-contained. Although in many local authority districts the number of people who crossed their boundaries every day was over 20 per cent of their resident populations, these areas were concentrated in and around the major urban centres. By 1951 districts with this intensity of movement covered a broad axial belt stretching from Lancashire to the south coast of England, and were also found in substantial blocks of South Wales and north-east England. The amount of movement in 1951 was greater in nearly every local authority area in England and Wales; and particularly noticeable was the degree to which the conurbations had become foci in a pattern of extensive daily movements.

The Rural–Urban Fringe

One feature of the modern city, in which the journey to work plays an important part, is the absence of a clear break between rural and urban conditions measured both in terms of land use and of social organization. Instead a rural–urban fringe zone is formed, in which various rural and urban characteristics are mixed together.

Until recently this transitional zone could be recognized on social grounds, with the fringe being notable for the presence of separate rural and urban groups, each with distinctive occupations and attitudes. Modern methods of communication, including radio and television as well as means of moving people and goods, are making the distinction between rural and urban social attitudes much less clear. Even occupations provide an imperfect guide, since with easier methods of travel both rural and urban jobs may be undertaken within the confines of the same family group. As a result, in large parts of western Europe and North America the impact of urbanism on social life extends well away from the immediate vicinity of cities and, from this point of view at least, it is no longer completely valid to recognize a rural–urban fringe.

Land use is perhaps a simpler criterion to apply; yet here again there are difficulties, springing from the essentially mixed character of the fringe zone. A casual inspection of the landscape is likely to produce an underestimate of the degree to which urban influences prevail in the environs of a large city. Some of the land uses may give a false impression of rurality, as where a village has become the home of a community of commuters. Or again, even land which is not built upon may have a very real urban function. Around large cities there are considerable areas of public open space—for example, common land used for recreation, or semi-public land like playing fields and golf courses.

In the rural environs of a large city the amount of land used for transport is above the average for a typical rural area, since here road and rail routes converge and these routes must have the capacity to carry commuters as well as long-distance traffic. In the nineteenth century railway marshalling yards were located on urban fringes, but now they have usually been swallowed up by later urban growth. On the other hand, airports are such recent additions to the pattern of communications that they are still located in the fringe zone. In some cases the earliest airports around cities have become surrounded by houses and, because they have been unable to extend their runways to meet the increasing demands of modern aircraft, they have been taken over for other urban purposes.

The fringe also attracts various uses which are necessary for the proper functioning of an urban settlement but would be less desirable within its actual built-up area. For obvious reasons sewage works and pumping stations fall into this class, and service reservoirs, which demand much space but must be close to a city, provide a further example. Provided suitable deposits are found, gravel workings may be taken as another instance, since their products are necessary for the urban construction industry but, because of the costs of transporting these bulky materials, cannot be hauled long distances.

Even where planning controls are strong, various distinctive types of land use are found in the urban fringe. To start with, it is very difficult and expensive to remove land uses which were established before planning control began to operate. Around London, for example, there is much building from pre-war days in the Green Belt. There are also certain uses which have been established recently, but allowed because they are considered appropriate on the urban fringe. Schools, hospitals, cemeteries and recreational land are all of this type; and, indeed, these uses are attracted by the fact that land values are kept down by the refusal to permit residential development.

In those countries where there is no effective control over the areas which are built upon, a further series of features are added to the rural–urban fringe. Around a city with an expanding economy and population, the fringe is a zone where land use may be expected to change sooner rather than later and land values are rising in expectation of this change. Where compact development is not enforced builders are often tempted away from the immediate vicinity of the city, either because of some intrinsic attraction of the site which they are developing, or because the higher costs of land adjacent to the built-up area encourages them to go farther away. As a result, unused spaces of varying sizes are left in the fringe zone, which are only gradually filled up.

The influence of cities is not limited to urban land uses. In the early nineteenth century the broad zone of agricultural land around a city often specialized in the production of milk and vegetables. These products were perishable and transport was relatively slow, hence a location close to an urban market was essential. Since then this tendency has been of decreasing importance, as means of transport have been improved and methods of food preservation have been perfected. With the greater flexibility of road transport, those environmental factors favouring specialist production are taking on greater importance than mere proximity to the urban market.

Immediately around the edge of the built-up area of a city another influence on land use makes its influence felt. Here there is a tendency for agricultural land to drop out of cultivation, sometimes because of the presence of non-rural residents, with their tendency to leave gates open and keep troublesome dogs, and partly because of the division of land into uneconomic units as patches are sold off for urban development. One further reason for the absence of cultivation is that land is being kept available for immediate disposal to speculators when the most appropriate moment arrives: the possibility of being able to sell a piece of land at the right moment more than compensates for the loss of the agricultural return over a short period.

The Limitation of Urban Spread

The indistinct boundary between urban and rural land use commonly found in the urban fringe can be avoided where development plans are devised in advance of the land actually being required for urban purposes. This "planned" situation itself produces a different series of repercussions. One result is that not much land is likely to lie dormant, unused either for rural or urban purposes, since the areas where building will be allowed are well known for some time ahead. Where urban development does take place, it is less likely to be in separate unrelated patches, as a definite edge to the built-up area can be preserved if permission to build is given in a logical sequence.

There will also be indirect effects springing from the control of outward growth. A city, whose built-up area is expanding rapidly, is likely to have a dynamic economy encouraging its growth. If a free market exists, the limitation of urban spread in such a situation will encourage land values to rise on those sites where permission to build has been granted. As a result the densities at which new development takes place are also likely to rise. In addition, land values will rise within the existing built-up area and, in suitable circumstance, this will also encourage changes.

For example, rising values may make the redevelopment of slum properties economically worth while, although in most cities this is not a profitable venture and is usually undertaken with government assistance of one kind or another. Where older properties stand in substantial gardens more profitable changes can be made. In modern London, for instance, considerable changes are taking place in the older middle-class suburbs, built in the late nineteenth century. The large gardens of the older houses have often been divided to provide sites for individual houses; and some houses have been converted into flats. Other houses have been completely demolished to provide valuable land for new dwellings, usually in the form of maisonettes or, if there is enough space to allow a large development, in flats.

Where the expansion of a large city has been checked and its increasing population cannot be accommodated by higher densities of building and by redevelopment, further urban growth is liable to be forced sufficiently far away from the central city to avoid the most vigorous planning restrictions. In London recent urban expansion has been particularly rapid beyond the outer limits of the Green Belt. The net result of this process is to produce longer and more wasteful journeys to work, but little real check is given to the general amount of urban expansion in the region around the conurbation.

It may be said, therefore, that the physical restriction of urban growth produces both good and bad results. From an aesthetic point of view there is much to be said for creating a less tenuous edge to urban development and for building new suburban houses at higher densities than have been common in the first half of the twentieth century. There are also practical advantages. For example, the limitation of urban expansion is likely to encourage greater attention to the layout and design of new houses. It may be, too, that the great expanse of very large cities demands more expenditure than necessary in travelling and creates wasteful congestion at critical points in the transport network, although many of these costs pass unnoticed because they are borne by the community rather than by the individual. Hence there is something to be said for keeping urban size within limits, although at our present state of knowledge it is difficult to say what these precise limits should be.

On the debit side is the likelihood that land values will be forced up by a simple restriction on urban expansion, thus pushing up the cost of housing and, in turn, the cost of living. In addition, once a pattern of control has been established vested interests also develop, anxious either to maintain or to alter the existing limits to urban growth. The political pressures which are thus created are not always in the interest of good planning administration. In particular, the owners of houses at the outer edge of urban expansion are often loath to see a further extension of the built-up area; and most owner-occupiers would be dismayed by the drop in land values which might be caused by the release of a substantial area of building land on the urban fringe. As a result a very inflexible attitude to the control of urban development is often created. Finally, it is unlikely that a policy of limiting urban growth will be successful unless the economic expansion of a growing city is also checked.

It is certainly debatable whether a complete check on the economy of a successful city would be a wise step; and it can be argued that a compromise, involving a combination of policies, would be not only prudent but desirable. Rather than completely prevent urban growth in a metropolitan region, one possible line would be to keep the central city in check, but to allow further development in a series of satellite centres. These centres would derive economic advantages from the presence of the central city, and the amount of daily travel necessary would be reduced. At the same time life would be socially more desirable than in endlessly sprawling suburbs and the visual appearance of town and countryside would be more acceptable. Following this same policy, it would also be necessary to examine the economic base of a growing metropolitan area to separate out those activities which benefit from a location in or close to the major city and those whose location is fortuitous and could be moved elsewhere.

Whether the growth of a city is completely restricted, steered into a prearranged framework, or allowed to proceed unimpeded, it is impossible to prevent all urban uses from penetrating the rural–urban fringe. The development of land for recreation is often a desirable process, to be encouraged rather than prevented; the use of land for transport and other purposes essential for the functioning of the city is inevitable. In no circumstances can the influence of a city be restricted to its built-up area; and even the limitation of residential expansion depends on the economic as well as on the physical planning of the urban area.

Selected Reading

For a description of suburban growth in London between the two world wars see

J. H. Johnson, The suburban expansion of housing in London, 1918–1939, in J. T. Coppock and H. C. Prince (eds.), *Greater London* (London, 1964), pp. 142–66.

A popular account of suburban growth in the United States during the twentieth century is

F. L. Allen, The big change in suburbia, *Perspectives* no. 9 (Autumn, 1954), 60–81. Also published in *Harper's* June 1954, 21–8 and *Harper's* July 1954, 47–53.

See also

H. J. Gans, *The Levittowners: How People Live and Politic in Suburbia* (New York, 1967).

Features of nineteenth-century middle-class suburbs are described in WARNER, *Streetcar Suburbs* (listed in the readings for Chapter 2) ; and for modern American cities a classic study is

H. HOYT, *The Structure and Growth of Residential Neighbourhoods in American Cities* (Washington, 1939).

Hoyt has returned to this theme in

Where the Rich and the Poor People Live, Technical Bulletin no. 55, Urban Land Institute (Washington, 1966).

A recent study of the same theme in some smaller English towns is to be found in

R. JONES, Segregation in urban residential districts: examples and research problems, in K. Norborg (ed.), *Proceedings of the I.G.U. Symposium in Urban Geography, Lund 1960* (Lund, 1962), pp. 433–46.

On squatter settlements see

D. J. DWYER, The problem of in-migration and squatter settlement in Asian cities: two case studies, Manila and Victoria—Kowloon, *Asian Studies* **2** (1964), 145–69.

On the distribution of shops within a typical American city see

M. J. PROUDFOOT, City retail structure, *Economic Geography* **13** (1937), 425–8.

This article is now somewhat dated, and for a more recent account see

J. E. VANCE Jr., Emerging patterns of commercial structure in American cities, in K. Norborg (ed.), op. cit., pp. 485–518.

A well-illustrated description of suburban shopping centres is given in

J. P. REYNOLDS, Suburban shopping in America: notes on shopping developments in the United States and the implications for Britain, *Town Planning Review* **29** (1958), 43–59.

The shopping centres of suburban London are examined by

A. E. SMAILES and G. HARTLEY, Shopping centres in the Greater London area, *Transactions of the Institute of British Geographers* no. 29 (1961), 201–13.

Daily travel in suburban London is examined in

J. WESTERGAARD, Journeys to work in the London region, *Town Planning Review* **28** (1957), 37–62.

The changing pattern of the journey to work in England and Wales is discussed by

R. LAWTON, The journey to work in England and Wales: forty years of change, *Tijdschrift voor Economische en Sociale Geografie* **54** (1963), 61–9.

The influence of commuters on rural surroundings is discussed in

F. I. MASSER and D. C. STROUD, The metropolitan village, *Town Planning Review* **36** (1965), 111–24; and
R. E. PAHL, *Urbs in Rure: the Metropolitan Fringe in Hertfordshire* (London School of Economics, 1965).

A convenient summary of the influence of the "Green Belt" idea around London is given in

D. THOMAS, The Green Belt, in J. T. Coppock and H. C. Prince (eds.), *Greater London* (London, 1964), pp. 292–312.
See also D. THOMAS, *London's Green Belt* (London, 1970).

Alterations to the geography close to a city in advance of actual building are discussed
in

J. D. FELLMAN, Pre-building growth patterns in Chicago, *Annals of the Association of American Geographers* **47** (1957), 59–82.

CHAPTER 8

MANUFACTURING AREAS IN CITIES

MANUFACTURING, like other land uses within cities, tends to be found in distinctive areas, but often exhibits a more complex arrangement than many other urban activities. This is because manufacturing includes a number of different types of production, the location of each being controlled by different combinations of factors. Accessibility (measured in a number of different ways), the history of urban development, the external economics which result from industrial groupings, these and other factors influence the distribution of industry within urban areas; but their relative importance varies from industry to industry.

The Attraction of Large Cities for Industry

The rise of industrial districts within cities is most clearly seen in the largest urban settlements, which in the twentieth century also offer the greatest attraction for a wide range of industrial enterprises. The casual visitor to a great capital often fails to realize that such cities are the most important centres of manufacturing within their countries. Greater London, for example, forms the outstanding manufacturing region in Britain and, indeed, possessed that status even in the middle of the nineteenth century, when the dark satanic mills of the coalfields provided the generally accepted image of industrial activity. In the same way Paris is the most important industrial centre of France, Dublin of Eire and New York of the United States, to quote just a few examples.

One of the most important factors attracting manufacturing to large cities of this kind is the accessibility to potential customers which their location provides. In fact the urban market for industrial goods possesses a number of different facets. Most obvious is the concentration of large numbers of people within the limits of a large city, either forming a market for certain mass-produced goods or providing enough specialized purchasers to support the manufacture of more esoteric products. A large city also provides accessibility to the many other potential customers located within its extensive zone of influence. But most firms sell their products to other manufacturers, rather than to the public at large, either for further processing or for assembly into larger items. Here again the large city provides an attractive location, because of the presence of numerous other industrial undertakings. Finally, as many large cities are ports, a location within them offers access to international as well as internal markets.

Industry is also attracted by the various external economies made possible in large cities. Many of the manufacturing firms which are typical of large cities form relatively small units and so depend on the services of independent concerns like transport operators and advertising agencies, which are more readily available in such a location. Or again, nearness to the sources of ideas and fashions is important for many urban industries, in particular those in which the detailed specification of their products changes frequently. Immediate awareness of the demands of the market is provided by a location in those centres where the trends of fashion are set. Possibly most important of all, the proximity of related industrial plants allows the processes of manufacture to take place more smoothly.

A third element in the attraction of large cities is the availability of a suitable labour supply, both skilled and unskilled. For specialized processes the large city provides a pool of skilled labour which, if not unemployed, at least can be attracted from other firms. In any case, the presence of other firms in the same line of business means that there are also likely to be facilities available for training skilled workers. In addition, the educational and cultural facilities of a large city makes it easier for manufacturers to recruit suitable staff for managerial jobs.

Major cities also offer a supply of unskilled labour, a fact which is not always made clear by the level of unemployment, which often tends to be below average in the larger cities of the Western world. For one thing, large cities form important points of attraction for immigrants, who are often available for less attractive, but essential, jobs. Such was the case in the clothing industry of the East End of London in the nineteenth century, which profited in particular from the Jewish immigration of the 1880's. In major cities, too, married women are available for certain types of work, sometimes part-time and sometimes arranged in shifts which allow them to combine housework with industrial employment.

The relative importance of these various factors varies from city to city and is not necessarily the same for an established as for a pioneering industry. Table 3 examines the results of a study of the industries of Greater New York, and lists the dominant factors which originally attracted manufacturers to this area. Studies of this kind are always somewhat unsatisfactory: the manager of an established firm does not always know the reasons for its original location and, in any case, the isolation of a dominant factor is often both difficult and arbitrary. Even so, Table 3 gives some indication of the relative importance of the factors attracting industry to a large city and allows a comparison with manufacturing industry in the United States as a whole.

One interesting feature of this table is the reduced importance of transport costs in the New York Metropolitan Area in comparison with all of the United States. Many of the industrialists in Greater New York sell their products to the local market and hence probably do not consider transport a dominant locating factor, although, by implication, it must be very important because of the large urban market immediately at hand. Goods sold to the national market are of greater value in relation to their bulk than the average industrial product, making transport costs much less significant for this sector of New York's industry than in the nation as a whole. Labour costs and supply are equally important in the New York Region and in the United States, but more detailed analysis indicates the importance of a skilled labour supply in the large city. Unskilled labour does not appear as a dominant attraction, but at the same time industrial expansion could not have taken place without its availability. Finally it should be noted that external economies stand out as the greatest force attracting industry to New York, and it is likely that this is true of all very large cities.

TABLE 3. LOCATIONAL FACTORS FOR MANUFACTURING INDUSTRY IN THE NEW YORK METROPOLITAN AREA, 1954 (AFTER R. LICHTENBERG)

Dominant locational factor	% of total manufacturing population	
	New York Region	All U.S.A.
Inertia	12·8	13·9
Transport costs	26·7	50·8
To sectional or local market	12·8	14·9
To national market	13·9	35·9
Labour costs and supply	8·2	8·1
For skilled labour	7·4	3·5
For unskilled labour	0·8	4·6
External economies	38·9	14·7
Unclassified	13·4	12·5
Total	100·0	100·0

Source: R. M. Lichtenberg, *One-tenth of a Nation* (Cambridge, Mass., 1960), table 3, p. 39.

Industrial Areas Close to the City Centre

The manufacturing function of cities is most noticeable where factories are grouped in suburban industrial estates or where a number of large plants form a zone of heavy industry along some line of bulk transport. In many cities, however, a major industrial area is located close to the city centre. Sometimes this area is interdigitated with the

FIG. 45. Major industrial areas of Greater London. (*Source*: Martin, in Coppock and Prince (eds.), *Greater London* (1964), p. 247.)

major shopping streets; sometimes it forms a separate industrial quarter close to the city centre. In London, for example, there is a distinctive industrial zone, which forms a crescent around the central area, particularly to the north and to the east. Outliers of this belt are found south of the Thames and there are also off-shoots from the crescent, where specialized industrial districts have grown up (Fig. 45). This inner industrial zone lies completely within the continuous built-up area of London at the end of the nineteenth century; and the "Victorian Manufacturing

Belt", as Peter Hall has called it, is still the major industrial area of the conurbation, although its relative importance has declined as a result of the modern growth of manufacturing in outer London.

Certain features are common to the industries of the inner areas of cities, in spite of the great diversity of products which are manufactured there. In particular the small manufacturing unit is typical of the inner industrial areas. Not only are factories small, but they use relatively little power in their operations, and firms with more than one factory are quite rare. As a result it is difficult to make economies of scale within the confines of a single firm, thus making the external economies produced by industrial grouping all the more significant in this kind of area.

Another special feature of these industries is the frequency and speed with which details of their individual products change, with careful supervision being needed for manufacturing routines, which are often altered after a short period. Skill in design and production is of more importance than investment in elaborate machinery or specially built factories, with the result that these small industrial plants are often located in converted buildings taken on a short lease. Industry is not an exclusive function of these inner manufacturing districts, but is mixed with warehouses, shops and residential accommodation of various kinds. Often these inner industrial areas form the zones of "blight" observed by urban sociologists, where delinquency and crime rates are high and slum attitudes prevail.

For some of these industries, too, the location of their factories close to the city centre is important in providing close links with customers. For example, clothing factories, especially those producing non-branded goods which are not nationally advertised, profit from a location close to large city shops. So, too, do jobbing printers, who cater for the day-to-day needs of offices and other central enterprises. Custom-made furniture and certain branches of precision engineering also find a location close to the city centre useful for the same kind of reasons.

The manufacture of women's clothing provides a particularly good example of the kind of manufacturing which takes place close to the centres of metropolitan cities. Success in this business cannot simply be bought by investment in factories and machinery; salesmanship and design are two particularly valuable assets in the "rag trade". A third important ingredient for a profitable clothing firm is flexibility in production, since although the total demand for women's clothing can be estimated reasonably accurately, the unpredictable demand for particular styles means that individual entrepreneurs must possess the utmost flexibility in production. Flexibility and specialized skills in selling, design and production are obtained by the subdivision of production among separate firms, which are closely grouped together in distinct areas of a city because of the need for close contact among them.

In New York, for example, there are three types of clothing firms, concentrated on about 150 acres of Manhattan. First there are the "manufacturers" who buy cloth, make garments and also sell them. Only about a quarter of the total number of clothing establishments are manufacturers: the remainer is made up of "jobbers" and "contractors". Jobbers buy cloth and design garments, but do not actually make them. Instead this job is carried out by the contractors, who produce to a specification and are not concerned with the marketing of the finished goods. In addition, such ancillary activities as the manufacture of buttons, zip fasteners and accessories are also carried out by independent firms. This division of production relieves manufacturers of the need to maintain factories which are large enough to fill peak orders, since with this system it is easy to let work out on sub-contracts. Similarly, each jobber can find additional contractors when the orders for his particular styles rise, and each contractor is not dependent upon the business of any one jobber, but may look elsewhere if insufficient work is coming in.

The kinds of product made in these inner manufacturing areas vary with the industrial history of individual cities and often reflect the nature of industrial expansion during the second half of the nineteenth century. Yet it would be wrong to ascribe their modern existence merely to the survival of a past situation. In some cases, certainly, the industries of the inner manufacturing areas represent relict features, which have little reason for their presence there today and are now in process of decay. For example, the gun quarter of Birmingham is shrinking in size, partly as a result of air-raid damage and the purchase of land for new municipal uses, but also because of foreign competition and the declining market for sporting guns. Or again, the watch and clock-making industry of inner London, which formed a flourishing industrial quarter in Clerkenwell in 1861, has left only a few traces today, as a result of competition from Swiss goods in the late nineteenth century.

Other, more fortunate, trades have expanded, but this very expansion has driven certain kinds of manufacturing out to suburban locations, as mass-production methods have demanded both more space for production and easier accessibility for motor vehicles. But other types of manufacturing have remained and flourished as a result of the continuing advantages of the inner industrial quarters for their activities, with subdivision of manufacturing and contact with buyers still being of vital importance to them. For example, although the precise limits of the jewellery quarter of Birmingham have altered considerably over the years, this still remains an active and prosperous industrial district. Or

in London, the clothing industry continues to flourish in the West and
East Ends; and the precision engineering quarter near Camden Town
has developed in the twentieth century to serve the needs of modern
technology, partly using the skills of men trained in the decayed clock
and watch-making industry of the same area.

The Expansion of Suburban Manufacturing

Although many of the light industries of the nineteenth-century city
were located quite close to the city centre, new manufacturing plants in
the twentieth century have become increasingly located in suburban
areas. Various factors were involved in this change in location, which
also affected the form of industrial areas and the size of individual
plants, but two forces in particular were important.

One was the changing nature of transport, which was altering patterns of accessibility within cities. Road traffic has always been important in the functioning of urban areas; but the coming of the motor-
car and the motor-truck, together with the rapid physical expansion of
cities, created a new situation. As the amount of road traffic grew, the
industrial areas around the centres of cities became increasingly congested, making them less satisfactory locations for those industries which
depended on large, regular flows of goods into and out of their factories.
As a result there was a strong encouragement for some plants to move
out to the suburbs (Fig. 46).

A second underlying force was the development of mass-production
techniques, which demanded space for the storage of parts and for the
proper layout of machinery, often in single-storey factories. Hence the
relatively cheap land of the suburbs and the space available there for
larger factories was also important in the growth of outlying industry;
and the new forms of transport allow a suburban factory to function
satisfactorily. The application of road transport to the inter-city movement of goods as well as to local cartage has reduced the pull of rail and
water terminals and allowed a suburban factory to supply a national as
well as a local market, and personal road transport by motor-car has
increasingly offset the difficulty of recruiting a suitable labour force in a
suburban site. Provided that their sites were made accessible by some
major road, new industrial establishments could be located on the fringe
of a major city and still recruit staff from a wide radius. At the same time,
suburban residential building was also taking place, with at least the
cheaper houses being closely associated with the new outlying industrial
estates.

The new suburban factories housed a varied assortment of enterprises, which had in common the fact that they were all industries which have expanded rapidly in the twentieth century. In some cases they were types of manufacturing which have had a long history in cities, but which were changing their scale of operations and their locations. Some branches of the printing industry provide an example of this, as does the expansion of the food-processing industries. The furniture industry also provides an instance: in London there was a migration of the cheaper "ready-made" furniture trade of the East End to larger factories in the Lea Valley. Similarly the high-class ready-made furniture trade of the Tottenham Court Road, at its peak in the late 1880's, now only survives in a few workshops attached to furniture retailers and a few surviving masters' shops, hidden away in small premises off the main roads. Instead, the output of this zone has been replaced by the expansion of new large factories in the outlying town of High Wycombe.

A second group of suburban industries are those which are making completely new products. Electrical engineering, for example, began to expand in the last quarter of the nineteenth century, but its massive growth has been a twentieth-century phenomenon. From its outset this industry has been dominated by the large, space-demanding factory; and between the two world wars suitable sites were to be found around the outer ring of London. Now, with increasing land values, new factories for this type of industry tend to be located up to 50 miles from central London, in order to find a suitable site at the right price.

Even among industries manufacturing new products there are a few examples of migration from the inner industrial areas. One case of this is the manufacture of radio receivers in the New York Metropolitan Area. In its early days this industry was characterized by small manufacturers, making a product which was still being modified rapidly and for which demand was uncertain and seasonal. As a result the pioneer firms in this business tended to choose a central location to obtain the flexibility which they needed. These firms employed a variable labour force of skilled workers and had relatively little capital tied up in expensive new plants and machinery, since this was then a highly speculative venture. Thus in its early days the manufacture of radio receivers was not unlike the women's fashion clothing industry and chose a similar kind of location. But during the late 1920's and 1930's a mass demand grew up for radio receivers, followed by a similar demand for television sets in the late 1940's, and when the industry settled down to large-scale production for a dependable market new locations were sought for large factories outside Manhattan.

The new suburban factories differed from the older industrial plants in that they were usually located on industrial estates, which, in a sense, were the equivalent of the shopping centres of the suburbs. Partly this sprang from the increasing emphasis in the twentieth-century city on zoning, with residential, commercial and industrial uses being kept in distinct areas by municipal ordinances. It also sprang from the activities of building developers, who saw the need for industrial estates, provided with attractive factories and with the necessary services for successful industrial activity. A classic example of the factory estate in Britain is provided by Park Royal, with over 330 acres of land being devoted to industrial uses. This estate grew from munitions factories, established during the First World War, which lay vacant in the 1920's. Served by road and railway, these buildings had an attraction for firms without capital to invest in specially built factories; and the developer of this industrial area soon began to add new standard factories, for which there proved to be a large demand.

Not all industrial estates were as large as this and the degree to which they represented carefully planned developments varied considerably. Some groups of new factories were simply stretched out along main roads, to form industrial estates with no aesthetic attraction but at least not intermixed with housing. In some cases the new suburban estates were a product of social rather than urban planning. During the 1930's in Britain, for example, some estates were built with government assistance to attract new light industries to areas where traditional industries were decaying. The Team Valley trading estate, three miles south of Newcastle-on-Tyne, was commenced in 1936 and provides an example of this kind of development. Here the intelligent layout of this group of factories indicates careful attention to overall design as well as the mere provision of factory floor-space to relieve unemployment.

A second general feature of twentieth-century suburban industry is the presence of larger working units than are found in the inner industrial areas. Indeed, this feature is an important reason for the choice of a suburban location. Yet, as always, average conditions tend to hide considerable detailed variations. The Park Royal estate illustrates this point well. On the edges of this industrial area, particularly to the north, there are very large factories, often concerned with the manufacture of food and drink, with labour forces measured in thousands. Towards the centre of the Park Royal estate, and therefore less obvious to the casual visitor, there are much smaller factories, employing less than 100 workers each and often engaged in general and electrical engineering. These smaller industrial plants, which are often located in rented factories, are not unlike some of those found in the older industrial districts, with a single firm being merely one link in a chain of industrial processes. Often, too, these factories have functional links with others on an estate, thus economizing on transport. The principal contrast with the inner industrial areas is that these smaller factories are housed in new buildings, segregated from other uses.

Indeed, perhaps it is easy to make too great a contrast between the suburban and inner industrial areas. Peter Hall has suggested that although they are morphologically very different, the factors which govern their location are basically similar. For both groups of industries the market and the pool of labour provided by a large city is important. Both derive external economies from being close to varied ancillary

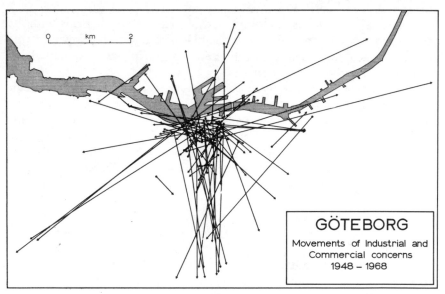

GÖTEBORG

Movements of Industrial and
Commercial concerns
1948 – 1968

FIG. 46. Movements of Industrial and Commercial Concerns in Göteborg, Sweden, 1948–1968. (*Source:* Dahl & Brånby, *Gothenburg in Maps* (1970), map 30.)

The map shows the movement of those firms that were members of the Göteborg Chamber of Commerce in 1948 and 1968. As the population of this city grew, many concerns moved from locations in and around its centre, partly because of increased congestion, partly because of higher land prices in the centre and partly because their activities demanded increased space.

industries and from being in close contact with new developments in fashion and technology. Even the possibility of renting ready-made factories in suburban industrial estates is paralleled by the possibility of acquiring workshops at relatively cheap rents in the decaying inner residential areas of cities.

The differences between the two types of area spring from the dates at which industrial expansion took place. The kinds of industry in a particular zone of a city often depend on the types of product which were in greatest demand when that period of urban growth was taking place. For instance, M. J. Wise has described how groups of factories established in Birmingham between 1860 and 1914 are found at a radius of some 2–3 miles from the city centre and are characterized by the manufacture and assembly of such products as bicycles, electrical apparatus and machine tools. Factories in the outer suburban ring of the city make products of recent origin, with the motor-car and aeroplane industries being particularly prominent. This temporal aspect has also been an important factor influencing the morphology of factories, since twentieth-century industrial growth occurred in an era when road transport was becoming more important, when ideas of land-use segregation were becoming more generally accepted, and when light industry was being organized in larger, more space-demanding units.

Industrial Areas Dependent upon Bulk Transport

A third type of urban industrial area is located close to harbour installations or some other means of handling bulky materials. Such industrial areas are not uncommon in cities, since many of the largest urban settlements are also ports. Nor is this type of area limited to coastal cities: the banks of important rivers and canals often attract the same kind of industrial area, if on a smaller scale. In large inland cities the development of heavy industries in association with railway transport facilities provides another example of the same general tendency.

A number of different kinds of manufacturing are found in this type of industrial area. One group of industries is concerned with the processing of imported raw materials. Sugar-refining and flour-milling are two typical examples, which serve both the urban centre itself and its hinterland. An industrial plant of this kind tends to be a large-scale operation, with labour charges taking only a relatively small proportion of the total costs and with a considerable amount of the weight of raw materials being "lost" in the process. Hence its most important requirement is for immediate access to a method of bulk transport. Moreover, bulk cargoes must be broken up at a port in any case, making this a suitable point for their further processing, in the midst of an urban market.

Oil-refining provides a similar example, with the break of bulk point again being a suitable point for the conversion of crude oil into various petroleum products. But as a result of considerations of safety, the noxious smell which the process involves and the need for extensive areas of cheap land for storage tanks, this industry tends to be located on the outskirts of a port city, perhaps on the shores of an estuary, rather than close to the centre. At present the growing importance of super-tankers is leading to the location of new refineries even farther away from cities, close to the few sites where ships with a displacement of over 100,000 tons can unload their cargoes. Pipelines, which offer relatively cheap transport inland, are also a contributing factor in the "outward" movement of oil terminals.

The manufacture of chemicals is another industry which has often been pushed out of the more central areas of cities by the nuisance caused by its processes, and which often depends upon methods of bulk transport. In London, for example, the lower Lea Valley is notable for a group of factories which make paint and varnish and blend oil and grease; near by are more factories which produce acids, iron oxides, acetates and similar products. The possibility of transporting raw materials by barge is an important element in the location of these industries.

Public utilities, like gas works and power stations, form another group of industries which are sensitive to bulk transport facilities. Power stations, for example, consume vast quantities of fuel, often most cheaply imported by water transport; and they also have large quantities of waste material which must be disposed of. Their need of water for cooling also confirms their waterside location. At least until recently, power stations and gas works have functioned most economically close to the areas where their products are used; hence public utilities have formed most important segments of the port industries of large cities.

Some factories in this kind of industrial area are not so much linked with transport facilities as with the other activities of the district. This is most clearly seen around a port, where many of the industries are concerned with serving shipping. The repair and maintenance of ships, and various branches of marine engineering find an obvious location alongside the harbour facilities of a major city. Another industry of the same kind is the manufacture of wire ropes and chains, while the manufacture of submarine cables provides an even more specialized example. Sometimes these industries have become more diversified with the passing of time, so that a whole range of light industries have also become associated with these areas. In London, for example, cable works located along various reaches of the Thames have turned eventually to the manufacture of switch gear, grid transmission cable and rubber products.

As many typical heavy industries depend on the nearby presence of raw materials and massive investment in manufacturing plant, their presence or absence in a city depends on the industrial context of a particular region. Shipbuilding, for example, is a distinctive port industry, demanding space and good transport links, but it is not found in every large port city. The manufacture of steel provides a similar example of an industry in which regional differences in the distribution of raw materials, the success of particular *entrepreneurs* and the availability of investment capital for certain forms of enterprise are particularly important. Allowing for these variations in industrial structure to which heavy industry is particularly sensitive, certain general features still

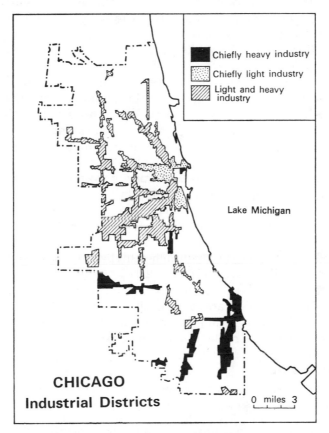

FIG. 47. Industrial districts in Chicago. (*Source*: Chicago Plan Commission, *Annual Report* (1944).)

The map shows the concentration of light industry close to the city centre, the location of more space-demanding industries farther from the centre along main traffic arteries, and the concentration of a specialized region of heavy industry in the Calumet district of south Chicago.

emerge about these industries which are orientated to means of bulk transportation.

In comparison with much other urban industry, for instance, these industries are usually organized in larger plants and carry out more self-contained operations. Often they are located together, not so much because of links between individual factories, but because they all depend upon ease of import (and, in some cases, export). There is also a tendency for individual plants to be sorted out by their demands for space and the degree to which they form noxious neighbours for other activities. This sorting process is partly a result of the influence of land values and partly because of zoning ordinances, which attempt to concentrate industries which are likely to create a nuisance into areas where they can do least harm.

It is more difficult to generalize about the distribution of this kind of industry within an urban area, since its location is greatly influenced by the site conditions in an individual city. For obvious reasons the location of navigable waterways, through railway routes and cheap, flat land are most important factors. Certainly the pressure of land values makes it unlikely that this kind of industry will be found close to a city centre, except possibly some types of manufacturing closely associated with the functioning of a seaport. Hence, in the last resort, the distribution of heavy industry in every individual city is more or less unique. In metropolitan New York, for example, the New Jersey coast is the location for many industries which can be classified as "heavy". Here there are diverse means of transport, with major highways, ocean shipping and railway marshalling yards all being accessible to industry. Here, too, there is flat open land, with relatively easy access to Manhattan. But the location of the industrial area is controlled by the special configuration of the site of New York, and it is difficult to fit it into any simple model of the urban structure of the metropolitan area.

Selected Reading

The attraction of one large city for manufacturing industry is discussed in

R. M. Lichtenberg, *One-tenth of a Nation: National Forces in the Economic Growth of the New York Region* (Cambridge, Mass., 1960).

A detailed analysis of three New York industries is made by

M. Hall (ed.), *Made in New York: Case Studies in Metropolitan Manufacturing* (Cambridge, Mass., 1959).

The changing pattern of industry in London is examined in

P. Hall, *The Industries of London since 1861* (London, 1962).

On this same general theme see

J. E. Martin, Three elements in the industrial geography of Greater London, in J. T. Coppock and H. C. Prince (eds.), *Greater London* (London, 1964), pp. 246–64; and P. Hall, Industrial London: a general view, ibid., pp. 225–45.

A case study of an inner industrial area of Birmingham is provided by

M. J. WISE, On the evolution of the jewellery and gun quarters in Birmingham, *Transactions of the Institute of British Geographers* no. 15 (1949), 57–72.

An economist's view of the distribution of urban industries is provided in

E. M. HOOVER, *The Location of Economic Activity* (New York, 1948), chapter 8, The economic structure of communities, pp. 116–41.

A planner's approach to the distribution of urban industry is provided by

G. LOGIE, *Industry in Towns* (London, 1952).

A geographer's classification of industrial locations within cities appears in

A. PRED, The intra-metropolitan location of American manufacturing, *Annals of the Association of American Geographers* **54** (1964), 165–80.

And for an American case study see

M. W. REINEMANN, The pattern and distribution of manufacturing in the Chicago area, *Economic Geography* **36** (1960), 139–44.

CHAPTER 9

THEORIES OF URBAN STRUCTURE

EVEN a casual inspection of cities reveals the existence of the various kinds of specialized areas which have been described in earlier chapters. It can also be sensed that there is repetition in the geographical arrangement of these different areas, reflecting such factors as land values, accessibility and the history of urban growth. As a result a number of theories have been devised which attempt to generalize about the arrangement of land use regions within a typical city.

The Concentric Theory

Much work in this field was associated with a group of urban sociologists who flourished in Chicago in the 1920's and 1930's. Thus the earlier generalizations about urban structure were designed to apply to cities in the United States, described conditions up to 40 years ago, and emphasized the interplay of urban environment and urban society within the various regions of a city. The most famous of these "models" of urban social areas was devised by E. W. Burgess in 1923 and has become known as the *Zonal* or *Concentric Theory*. This model is based upon the notion that the development of a city takes place outwards from its central area, to form a series of concentric zones (Fig. 48).

The zones begin with the Central Business District, which is surrounded by an area of transition. In this transitional zone older private houses are either in process of being taken over for offices and light industry, or are being subdivided to form smaller dwelling units. This is the area of the city to which immigrants are attracted, and it is characterized by "vice" areas and generally unstable social groups rather than by settled families. In turn the transitional zone is surrounded by the zone of working-men's homes. Here are found some of the older residential buildings in the city, but social groups are stable and largely consist of working-class families. Still farther from the centre newer and more

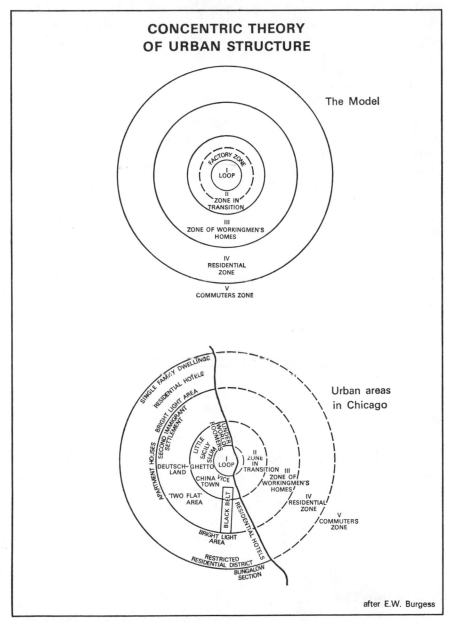

CONCENTRIC THEORY
OF URBAN STRUCTURE

The Model

FACTORY ZONE
I
LOOP
II
ZONE IN
TRANSITION
III
ZONE OF WORKINGMEN'S
HOMES
IV
RESIDENTIAL
ZONE
V
COMMUTERS ZONE

Urban areas
in Chicago

SINGLE FAMILY DWELLINGS
RESIDENTIAL HOTELS
BRIGHT LIGHT AREA
SECOND IMMIGRANT SETTLEMENT
APARTMENT HOUSES
LITTLE
SICILY
SLUM
DEUTSCH-LAND
GHETTO
UNDER WORLD
ROOMERS
LOOP
I
II
ZONE IN
TRANSITION
III
ZONE OF
WORKINGMEN'S
HOMES
IV
RESIDENTIAL
ZONE
V
COMMUTERS
ZONE
CHINA
TOWN
VICE
'TWO FLAT'
AREA
BLACK BELT
RESIDENTIAL HOTELS
BRIGHT LIGHT
AREA
RESTRICTED
RESIDENTIAL DISTRICT
BUNGALOW
SECTION

after E.W. Burgess

FIG. 48. The concentric theory of urban structure. (*Source*: Park, Burgess and
McKenzie (eds.), *The City* (1925), pp. 51–3.)

spacious dwellings are found, occupied by middle-class groups. Finally the commuters' zone lies beyond the continuous built-up area of the city, its outer limit being about one hour's travelling time from the city centre, where a considerable proportion of the population of this zone is employed. Much of the commuters' zone may still be open country, but the villages found within it are often changing their character to form dormitory settlements.

Although it has been widely used as a conceptual framework for studying urban areas, Burgess's theory has been severely criticized by later workers. Much of this attack has been somewhat unfair, since it has been based on a too literal interpretation of a theory which was always intended as a very broad generalization. For example, Burgess only expected his hypothesis to apply in the absence of "opposing factors", such as local topographical features, which might well influence the location of the best residential areas. Burgess also expected that there would be considerable variation within his various zones: local "natural areas", distinguished by the social, economic and demographic traits of their inhabitants, were to be expected within the broader zonal framework.

In practice, too, many cities show a star-shaped rather than a concentric form, with urban development pushing along the highways which radiate from their centres and with contrasting types or urban land use being found in the interstices between the main roads. Apologists for the Burgess theory have suggested that if such a city were re-mapped in terms of the time and cost of travelling to the centre, rather than of the linear distance involved, a concentric arrangement would be produced. If this view is correct, similar types of land use are likely to be found at the same journey time from the centre.

The theory has also been modified by the suggestion that identical urban regions are not to be expected in concentric zones, but merely that particular types of land use tend to occur at the same distance from the centre, often in patches rather than forming a continuous ring. This approach has developed into the statistical study of traverses from the city centre to the suburbs; but in studies of this kind the emphasis has been on economic rather than on sociological analysis and must be discussed later.

The Sector Theory

Even after suitable allowance has been made for its general character, there remain certain discrepancies between the concentric theory and reality, encouraging the postulation of other theories of urban structure. One of the most important of these is the *Sector Theory*, which was first advanced about 1939 and is frequently associated with the American land economist Homer Hoyt, although M. R. Davie put forward similar views about the same time. Hoyt's idea was that, once contrasts in land use had arisen near the centre of a city (perhaps originally as a result of mere chance), these differences were perpetuated as the city expanded. Distinctive sectors of land use were likely to grow out from the centre, often focused on major routeways (Fig. 49, A).

Certainly this idea of the wedge-like expansion of urban areas is an improvement on the earlier theory in that it pays more attention to the

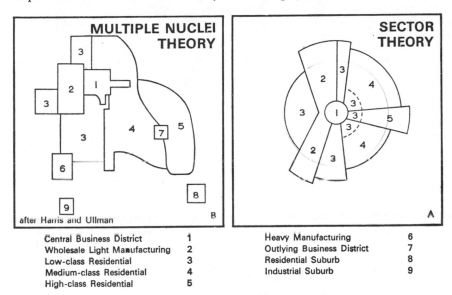

Central Business District	1
Wholesale Light Manufacturing	2
Low-class Residential	3
Medium-class Residential	4
High-class Residential	5

Heavy Manufacturing	6
Outlying Business District	7
Residential Suburb	8
Industrial Suburb	9

Fig. 49. The sector theory and the multiple nuclei theory of urban structure. (*Source*: Harris and Ullman, *Annals of the American Academy of Political and Social Science* **242** (1945), 13.)

importance of transport in the functioning of a city. Industry, which was given scant attention in the concentric theory, also fits better into this scheme of things. But the sector theory applies most appropriately to the development of residential areas. Once a district with high-class housing has been established, the most expensive sites for new houses will lie along the outer edge of this area. The net result over a period of urban expansion is that a zone of high-class housing tends to be located on one side of a city rather than in the continuous ring supported by the concentric theory.

Although better-class housing may extend outwards in a sector, at the same time the age of buildings is more likely to show a concentric

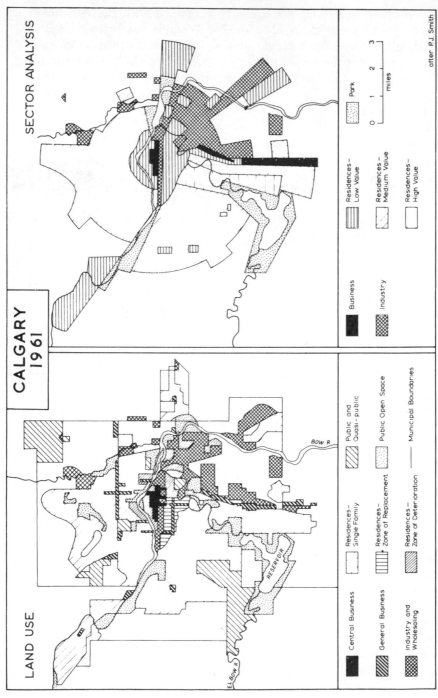

Fig. 50. Calgary, 1961: land use and its interpretation by sectors. (*Source:* Smith, *Economic Geography* **38** (1962), 318 and 328.)

arrangement, as layer upon layer of houses are added to the urban fringes. Hence it is probably better to look upon Hoyt's theory as a refinement rather than as a radical alteration of the earlier concentric

SHIFTS IN LOCATION OF FASHIONABLE RESIDENTIAL AREAS

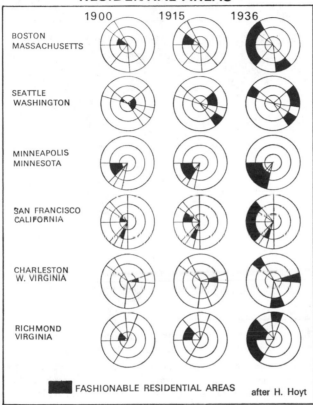

FIG. 51. Shifts in the location of fashionable residential areas. (*Source*: Federal Housing Administration, *The Structure and Growth of Residential Neighbourhoods in American Cities* (1939), p. 115.)

The illustration shows in diagrammatic form how "high rent" residential areas have migrated outwards over time in various United States cities.

model. Nor does it follow that a whole sector will be geographically similar at any one moment of time. The older, more central, buildings may well undergo change—for example, as a result of the social leap-frogging described in an earlier chapter. In a study of thirty American cities published in 1939, Homer Hoyt showed in diagrammatic form how high-rent areas, that is the best residential districts, migrated outwards (Fig. 51). In other words, these cities show elements of both a concentric and a sector structure.

The possibility of the coexistence of the two theories is also illustrated by Peter Mann's suggestion of the urban structure of the typical medium-sized British city, large enough to have considerable internal

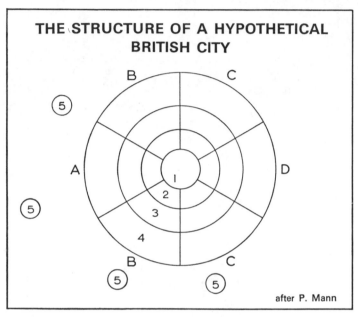

FIG. 52. The structure of a hypothetical British city. (*Source*: Mann, *An Approach to Urban Sociology* (1965), p. 96.)

This diagram assumes a prevailing wind from the west. Features of the model include: 1, the city centre; 2, transitional zone; 3, zone of small terrace houses in sectors C and D; larger bye-law houses in sector B; large old houses in sector A; 4, post-1918 residential areas, with post-1945 development mainly on the periphery; 5, commuting-distance "villages". A, the middle-class sector; B, the lower middle-class sector; C, the working-class sector (and main municipal housing areas); D, industry and lowest working-class sector.

differentiation, but not exhibiting the complications found in a conurbation (Fig. 52). Essentially his diagrammatic model combines the sector and concentric theories, with some allowance for commuting from distinct villages. Incidentally, the diagram assumes that the prevailing wind comes from the west, with the result that the best residential area is located on the western fringe of the city, on the opposite side from the industrial sector.

It should also be recalled that Hoyt applied his theory in quite a specialized manner to the assessment of the pattern of residential growth, rather than to the analysis of the total structure of the American city. As he was basically concerned with the history of residential development, Hoyt extracted from his general theory certain "rule-of-thumb" guides to the expected lines of future expansion. High-class residential areas, he suggested, might be expected to expand along established lines of travel in the direction of an existing nucleus of buildings. High-rent areas would tend to spread along higher ground or along waterfronts (if these were not already used by manufacturing industry). They were also likely to grow towards the homes of leaders of the community. But these economic and social forces were not inexorable, since he believed that real-estate speculators could bend the direction of high-class residential growth by skilful promotion.

The importance of "non-rational" factors of this kind has been further emphasized by Walter Firey, who would like this non-economic element built into any theory of urban structure. Firey cites the case of Beacon Hill in Boston, which has remained a high-class residential area for social reasons, rather than because of its location in the city. It is certainly true that the very wealthy can choose to live anywhere and, in particular circumstances, they may not follow the "normal" pattern, as described in the concentric and sector theories. The less well-off are more circumscribed by their economic situation and are thus more likely to fit into a repetitive pattern of urban structure based on accessibility, amenity and rent-paying ability.

The Multi-centred City

The concentric and sector theories have the advantage of attractive simplicity, but the situation in most cities is possibly too complex to be enfolded in such easily comprehended generalizations. As a result these theories have been elaborated, producing results which accord more closely with reality, but at the same time are less clear than the earlier statements. One example of this elaboration is the *Multiple Nuclei Theory*, which was advanced by two geographers, C. D. Harris and E. Ullman, in 1945. This theory suggests that cities have an essentially cellular structure, in which distinctive types of land use have developed around certain growing points, or "nuclei", within the urban area (Fig. 49, B).

The grouping of specialist land uses around these nuclei has been encouraged by four factors, which influence the distribution of human activities within a city in various ways. To start with, certain activities

require specialized facilities, either those found in the natural endow-
ment of their sites, or provided later by human endeavour. The location
of the Central Business District at the point of maximum accessibility
gives an illustration of this factor. Or again, certain activities group together because they profit from cohesion, an example being the clustering of the clothing industry in the inner districts of some large cities.
Other activities are detrimental to one another and are not normally
found in close juxtaposition: for example, heavy industry and high-class
residential areas are rarely near-neighbours. Finally, certain activities
are unable to afford the rents of the most desirable sites: the location of
areas of cheaper housing or bulk storage facilities provide examples of
this factor in operation.

The multiple nuclei idea allows for the fact that the internal geography of cities owes much to the peculiarities of their individual sites,
as well as to the operation of more general economic and social forces.
Yet even the nature of the detailed site operates within a framework provided by social and economic factors. An area with a well-drained,
wooded terrain often favours the development of a high-class residential
area, but this process also depends on the social assessment of what
constitutes a "desirable" environment for residential building and on the
location of the area in a section of the urban fringe which is ripe for
development. Similarly, heavy industry may be attracted by a flat,
ill-drained area (or, more precisely, by the cheap, extensive sites which
such an area offers), provided that suitable transport facilities are available and that this kind of industry is present in a particular city.

In the Multiple Nuclei theory, too, the history of individual cities is
also seen as an important factor shaping the form of urban development.
Harris and Ullman cite the case of central London, with the area of the
medieval city now providing the location for the most important financial activities and the area around the Palace of Westminster providing
the centre for political administration. But, again, more general economic and social factors are also operating, since internal specialization
within their central areas is a general feature of large cities; and the process of metropolitan growth, an important factor in the development of
central London, is also an international phenomenon. Whatever the
reasons for their origins, once nuclei for various types of activities have
been established, the general factors encouraging the sorting out of
urban activities into distinctive land use regions confirm and develop
the pre-existing pattern.

The unique element which is introduced by accepting the relevance of
historical and site factors means that the Multiple Nuclei theory cannot
produce a simple model of urban structure, immediately discernible

in the form of every city. Nor does this theory exclude the probability that elements of the concentric and sector arrangements will also be found in particular cities. Perhaps it is better to look upon this approach more as a guide to thought about the structure of the city, rather than as a rigid generalization about urban form.

Both the Concentric and Sector theories assume that a typical city will grow around a single centre; and even the diagram with which Harris and Ullman illustrated their Multiple Nuclei theory made the same assumption, although obviously their idea is applicable to more complex examples. In large modern cities, however, the distribution of retail shopping centres provides a more complicated framework for urban structure. These centres are usually arranged in the hierarchical pattern first formally described in Philadelphia by Malcolm J. Proudfoot*; and although most cities have only one central business district, they also have a series of sub-centres, which provide for the less specialized needs of smaller sections of the city.

Such an approach is only concerned with retail land use, but residential districts are grouped around these retail sub-centres, so that in the suburban areas of large cities there exists a many-centred pattern, which is at least partly independent of the influence of site and history. The net result is that reality appears to consist of what Amos Hawley has called "a constellation of centres, set upon a patchwork of small internally homogeneous areas".† It is this situation which allows various types of arrangements to be seen in the form of cities, whose detailed complexity reveals traces of a number of different models of urban structure.

Gradient Analysis

The various models of cities discussed so far consist of qualitative descriptions of the form of urban structure, but there have also been attempts to describe cities in quantitative terms. Most frequently quantitative techniques have been applied to what has been called *Gradient Analysis*. The idea behind this approach is that many features of a typical city tend to vary in a logical sequence at increasing distances from the centre. As a result graphs can be constructed to illustrate this progression, and equations can be calculated which, in turn, describe the graphs. The application of gradient analysis to the study of population density within the city has already been described in an earlier chapter,‡ but the same method can be applied to other economic and

* See Fig. 42, p. 142.
† Amos Hawley, *Human Ecology* (New York, 1950), p. 287.
‡ See Chapter 3, pp. 58–62.

social features. Gradient analysis, however, is not completely independent of the concentric and sector theories, since often the methods by which data are handled consciously or unconsciously assume the existence of these models. Conditions at various distances from the city centre are sometimes taken as the averages for a series of concentric zones; and sometimes the data are processed by individual sectors, often along the line of a highway.

Interest in gradient analysis has increased greatly during the last decade, stimulated by the work of the British economist Colin Clark, but it is by no means new. For example, although he does not appear to have influenced modern work, H. Bleicher analysed the distribution of population within Frankfurt am Main in 1892 and noticed a regular decline in density between the inner and outer residential areas.* As early as 1928 E. W. Burgess himself was referring to the various social and economic gradients produced by the growth of a city; and in 1929 C. R. Shaw examined the distribution of juvenile delinquency within urban areas, both in terms of zone gradients (measured by concentric circular zones) and radial gradients (measured along certain streets radiating from the urban centre). During the 1930's such features as the distribution of land values, the density of urban traffic and the proportion of land used for commercial purposes were subjected to this form of analysis.

In the early 1930's, too, Charles C. Colby published an influential paper in which he explored the logical basis of these various urban gradients. Colby recognized that two groups of forces underlay the contrasts between the centres and the peripheries of cities. One group, the centrifugal forces, drove out certain land uses from city centres because of the increased site costs and the congestion associated with a central location. The other group, the centripetal forces, attracted specialized land uses to city centres because of their accessibility to customers and the close proximity to closely related activities which could be obtained there.

The emphasis in these studies of urban gradients was somewhat different from that implicit in the three classical theories of urban structure. Basically, the Concentric, Sector, and Multiple Nuclei theories were all descriptions of the urban structure produced by the process of city growth. The studies of gradients, on the other hand, were more concerned with the interrelations among the various economic and social phenomena found in different parts of a city. This approach is now being given further impetus by the application of more advanced statistical

---

* H. Bleicher, *Statistische Beschreibung der Stadt Frankfurt am Main und ihrer Bevölkerung* (Frankfurt am Main, 1892).

techniques. For example, the relationships among various urban gradients can be explored by such statistical techniques as multiple regression analysis.

Certainly the study of urban gradients should produce a greater awareness of the ways in which the various social and economic phenomena found in a city are linked; but it has also been argued that distinctive gradients are associated with different forms of urban activities and that, if generalizations can be made about the form of these various gradients, it should be possible to produce quantitative "models" of urban structure. Unfortunately in practice this is proving a complicated task, since it now seems clear that the gradients from city centre to urban periphery are not as simple and orderly as was earlier supposed.

One source of this complication is the changes which are currently taking place in the modern city, with the result that a theory of urban structure which might have been appropriate for a city in the early 1920's is no longer applicable today. One important changing feature, with implications for the concentric theory as well as for gradient analysis, is the rise of suburban employment, first in manufacturing and now increasingly in retail distribution. When the first theories of urban structure were being advanced in the 1920's the impact of suburban manufacturing was not as great as it has now become; but by 1943 Chauncy Harris was able to show that a substantial proportion of the suburbs of American cities were not upper-class commuting areas and hence did not fit into the concentric model of urban structure. Currently, urban renewal in the United States is leading to the construction of more expensive dwellings close to city centres, displacing poorer citizens from these locations. Although this change perhaps may not greatly alter density gradients, it will certainly modify other social and economic gradients.

In Britain the picture is further complicated by the impact of administrative action. Here, for example, local authority housing estates have introduced working-class residents into formerly middle-class areas. Here, too, density gradients have been modified by land-use controls, which have been successful in producing a clearer distinction between town and country and have thus also produced a more clearly defined break in the population density gradient at the outer limit of built-up areas.

As a result of the decreasing validity of at least some of the classical theories, experimental work is now being carried out on new methods of analysing the spatial structure of cities. These new methods do not demand the acceptance of deductive theories of urban form as a basis for calculations. For example, Elizabeth Gittus has been studying

Merseyside and south-east Lancashire from this point of view, applying the technique of component analysis to the classification of regions within cities, in much the same way as it has been used to group cities into similar socio-economic types.* It remains to be seen whether an inductive method of this kind will produce generalizations about urban structure which will allow the valid comparison of different cities.

The Form of the Pre-industrial City

The changes taking place in the Western city are gradually invalidating at least some aspects of the earlier theories of urban structure. These changes are produced by alterations in the nature of society and technology: different social and technological contexts produce different urban forms. But these different contexts are not simply a product of change through time. There are also cultural variations in different parts of the world at any one point of time which may produce a variety of urban forms.

The comparison of the types of cities produced by different cultures is a matter of tentative investigations rather than firm generalization. Perhaps some would argue that it is difficult enough to formulate agreed generalizations within the limits of a single country, where similar aims and attitudes prevail, without the further complications provided by the varying goals of society in the world at large. The comparisons which have been made so far have usually been concerned with the contrasts between the Western city, produced by a capitalist society with a relatively free market in land, and the so-called "pre-industrial" city, found in societies which have urban life as part of their indigenous cultures but have so far been touched only lightly by the reorganization of society and economy brought about by the Industrial Revolution.

Such a simple contrast must be an over-simplification. The cities of the U.S.S.R., for example, do not fit neatly into this classification, although they form a sub-species of the Western city, being based on a modern industrial economy. Or again, the cities of Latin America are difficult to classify in this way. Some are modern Western cities in the true sense of the term; but the smaller, more isolated, towns are a product of a pre-industrial economy, although they may owe their origins to west European settlers. In spite of the difficulties of definition Gideon Sjoberg has suggested that the pre-industrial city has a distinct form, which is repeated in a wide range of cultures, areas and times. This similar morphology can be distinguished in both general and detailed features of pre-industrial cities.

* See above, pp. 77–8

In general, past and present pre-industrial cities are small settlements, with a total population rarely over 100,000, and usually much less. This is not surprising, since these cities are set in relatively unurbanized societies, with often as little as 5 per cent of the total population living in towns. In addition, the food suppliers of pre-industrial cities are drawn from their immediate hinterlands; and with relatively inefficient means of moving bulky goods, these pre-industrial societies could only support small urban clusters.

Most of these cities, too, are surrounded by a wall, indicating the need for protection and a technology in which protection can still be obtained from such a device. The wall also indicates a clearer separation of rural and urban life than is found in Western society; it serves to control movement to and from the outside world, either for the collection of tolls or to ward off undesirables.

At first sight the congestion which is typical of the pre-industrial city also appears to be linked with the presence of an encircling wall, but the fundamental cause lies deeper than this. Methods of transport within most of these cities are such that people wish to reside and work where they have immediate access to the central facilities of the city. Movement is slower and mechanical transport is relatively more expensive than in Western cities, encouraging the development of compact cities which appear congested to Western eyes. Furthermore, the technology of these pre-industrial communities does not allow the construction of very tall buildings, with the result that houses are closely packed together along narrow streets, so as to obtain the advantages of proximity.

The detailed pattern of the pre-industrial city also shows contrasts with the typical Western city, particularly in the distribution of social classes. The upper classes, instead of living in the outer fringes of the city, tend to live close to the centre. Political and religious activities in pre-industrial societies often possess higher prestige than economic pursuits and play a more important part in the lives of the *élite*. As the citadels of Church and State are often located at the centre, and as transport within the city is often poorly developed, the upper classes must reside close to the centre if they wish to participate in the affairs of government and religion. On the other hand, the poorest citizens often live on the outskirts. Here are the only sites left for their occupation; and, in any case, many of the poor are employed in agriculture, an occupation which demands access to the open country around the city, or in noxious pursuits which are not tolerated within the built-up area.

A second detailed feature of many of these cities is their cell-like structure, based sometimes on occupations, but also on ethnic differences and family groupings. In the indigenous cities of western Nigeria, for example, the older residential areas are notable for their division into separate compounds, each of which is inhabited by the members of a very large extended family. A similar example is provided by the medieval cities of central Europe, which possessed distinctive quarters inhabited by ethnic groups different from the bulk of the population.

To the subdivision produced by social forces is added that caused by the greater measure of occupational specialization in different sections of the pre-industrial city. With poorer transport and less efficient exchange of information, the interaction between producers, middlemen and consumers takes place more smoothly if particular occupations are concentrated together. As a result individual streets have become associated with particular types of activity. Of course, groupings of this kind are found in the centres of modern Western cities, for much the same reason; but in the Western city this grouping applies to a much smaller range of specialized activities and only tends to be a noticeable feature in the central areas of the largest cities.

Yet although particular economic activities are grouped together, land uses do not exhibit the extreme specialization found in the modern Western city. Facilities for residence, work and other activities can all be found within the same small area of the city. Indeed, the same plot of land often serves multiple functions. A religious building, for example, may also serve as a school, with markets being held on the grounds around the building. Within the confines of the same building a man may reside, produce his wares, and also store and sell them, thus adding to the impression of congested confusion given by these pre-industrial cities.

Although a number of distinctive features can be found in preindustrial cities, it is open to dispute whether all these cities can be classified as belonging to the same type, since it is doubtful whether these repetitive features are always found in association within the confines of an individual city. Certainly some elements in their urban structure are repeated in a large range of cities, widely scattered in time and in place, largely because they have similar forms of transportation which control some elements of their internal form and limit the distances over which food to support the urban population can be moved. But it would be rash to claim that all have an identical technological and social basis, thus producing an identical morphology. Much comparative work will be required before this verdict of "not proven" can be modified into outright acceptance or rejection of Sjoberg's theory of the structure of the pre-industrial city.

The Dual Structure of Colonial Cities

In practice, however, comparison is made difficult by the manner in which Western influences have now penetrated most cities in the modern world. There are few urban settlements which have not been touched by these influences, although sometimes their effects are subtle—perhaps seen in changing rates of natural increase, rather than in any dramatic alteration in urban structure. On the other hand, where the introduction of Western culture has brought an economic revolution as well as new ideas, the interplay of contrasting cultures has had a more striking effect on the structure of the indigenous city.

Sometimes this influence has led to the building of new cities where none had stood before, their growth being based on the introduction of Western-style economic systems and transport networks. The structure of these new cities has more in common with the Western than with the indigenous city, but these planted settlements take on special characteristics as a result of the different social environment into which they have been introduced. An example is provided by Calcutta, which is functionally similar to a Western city, but is more compact than might be expected in an American or west European city of the same population. This compactness owes much to the fact that in Calcutta upper-class residential areas are found closer to the centre than would be expected in a typical Western city, for reasons which have probably more to do with the former segregation of European areas than with the functioning of transport.

The fact that some of these planted cities have been growing very rapidly in the midst of large, under-employed, rural populations has also encouraged the development of special features. In such a situation people are attracted by urban life only partly because of a positive economic "pull" from the city. A cash income has a seductive appeal for a struggling subsistence cultivator, and casual unskilled work for payment can be obtained more easily in these cities than in their economically underdeveloped hinterlands. As a result these urban areas attract a large number of people to a meagre existence which would have little appeal in the Western world. These very poor people can find homes only on unused land on the urban fringes, where they have squatted in shanty towns. Around many of the most rapidly growing cities of Latin America the presence of squatter settlements of this kind is a common feature, and they are also found around some of the most Westernized cities of Asia.*

The result of the interaction of Western and native cultures is most clearly seen where a basically Western city has been grafted to a

* See also pp. 18–19 and 140–1

pre-existing indigenous city. "Mixed" cities of this kind are not an uncommon feature of the former colonial countries where old and new urban developments have been juxtaposed and serve as a visible indication of the distinctiveness of two cultures.

The old city of Delhi, for example, is surrounded by walls and the remains of a moat. Within the walls there is a high density of buildings, which are used for both residential and commercial purposes, the streets show an irregular pattern and dwellings are arranged around central courtyards. Outside the old city lie modern shops and offices, the equivalent of the Western Central Business District, a railway quarter, and modern residential areas. Here, too, are such features as a spacious governmental area and a military cantonment, both survivals of the British Raj. In fact, what is found here is a fossil of a pre-industrial city embedded in a modern Western city. In Pakistan, Lahore serves as a very similar example, with the same features—the old city, a modern commercial area, the cantonment, a railway quarter and modern residential areas.

In Africa north of the Sahara the same phenomenon is seen in the European and Moslem quarters of former colonial cities, but in Tropical Africa an indigenous urban tradition was largely absent. Only in West Africa are there a few examples: Akin Mabogunje has described the structure of Ibadan in western Nigeria, now a city with more than 600,000 people. Here an African town grew during the nineteenth century, before European influence became effective. Again the interplay of two cultures can be seen in the morphology of the town. Although the town wall has now gone, within its former limits is an area with high residential densities, inhabited by a population of local origin, with commercial activity in the form of traditional markets. The modern commercial and government areas are located on one side of this core. The outer zones of the city include the homes of immigrants from elsewhere in Nigeria as well as from overseas; and they also include areas devoted to modern educational uses (Fig. 53).

Comparative studies which examine cities like these should recall that what is being studied is not one city, but an amalgam of two. For example, gradient analyses, using simple traverses from the city centre, may possess little validity in a city with a dual structure of this kind. Similarly, more general comparative studies are complicated by the fact that the social and economic interaction between the residents of the two sections depends greatly on local circumstances.

Indeed, an awareness of local circumstances is always important for the understanding of the urban geography of a particular area. Different societies make varying assessments of what constitutes an amenity,

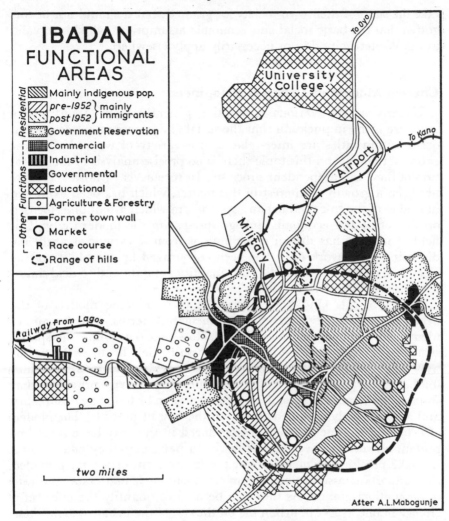

Fig. 53. The functional areas of Ibadan. (*Source*: Mabogunje, *Yoruba Towns* (1962), p. 14.)

different technologies produce distinctive patterns of accessibility, and different assumptions about the nature of land-ownership cause variations in the operation of the urban land market. As a result the detailed structure of a typical city may well vary from culture to culture, and the factors which explain its form may also differ in emphasis. Research workers trained in the large cities of the Western world can perhaps take the *mores* of their own society for granted; but it should not be forgotten that the basic social and economic assumptions which are valid in the Western city do not necessarily apply elsewhere.

Current Models of Urban Development

Underlying the various descriptive generalizations about urban structure is the implication that the social and economic processes that occur within cities are inter-related in a variety of ways; but in the classic statements on this topic there is no precise analysis of the operation of these interdependent processes. In recent years, however, there has been a growth of interest in this matter, which has been expressed in studies of the so-called urban "system", in which attention is focused on the social and economic linkages present in the modern city. This field of interest has drawn contributions from a variety of academic disciplines, and work on it has been encouraged by the ability of the electronic computer to handle vast quantities of data and to deal simultaneously with many variables.

Studies of this kind have proceeded by producing models of the urban system, usually couched in mathematical terms, with the aim of identifying the maze of interacting factors that determine the spatial structure of cities. In theory at least, these models begin with various hypotheses about the functioning of cities, which are translated into mathematical statements of various forms. In turn, provided that suitable data are available, these statements can be tested against reality and appropriately modified to obtain the best fit possible. The models of urban development which are produced in this way have some important advantages over earlier work. In particular they can be used to make precise statements about the future form of a city, provided that important assumptions are made about such matters as the rate of population change. As they can be used to quantify the effect of a change in one aspect of urban life on the rest of the urban system, these models can also be employed to evaluate the effects of planning policies, since they make it possible to explore the ramifications that particular decisions are likely to have throughout a whole urban system.

These statistical models that can be used for planning purposes have often had their origin in the United States, with the result that they are based on assumptions which reflect conditions in western cities, with a relatively free market in urban land. As a consequence they are at present difficult to apply convincingly in other contexts. For example, there are problems in adapting them for cities in command economies, where state decisions play a detailed role in day-to-day life. Even greater difficulties arise in cities associated with non-western traditional societies, since the aspirations of the individual urban dweller may well be different from those held in the western world and, as a result, such matters as the choice of desirable locations for various urban activities may also be different.

It must also be recorded that, even if attention is limited to a strictly western context, some of the models that are currently being used may show considerable statistical sophistication but in fact do not reflect any greater theoretical grasp than was present in earlier generalizations about the spatial pattern of urban life. It is clear, too, that most models embrace only a limited segment of the total spectrum of the city, although, in fairness, it is only through simplification of the complexity of reality that progress can be made in unravelling the most important strands in the pattern of human activities within large cities.

The detailed strategies that can be adopted in model design cannot be explored here, but something of the range and content of these models can be indicated by a brief examination of three different examples of the kind of work that has been undertaken. These examples should also serve to illustrate the possibilities and limitations of this approach.

Some of the earliest work in this field has been associated with transport planning, since it has for long been recognized that different land uses generate distinctive amounts and types of traffic and that, at the same time, changes in transport facilities strongly influence parallel changes in urban land use. One well-known and well-documented example is the method devised about 1960 by the Chicago Area Transportation Study for forecasting land uses in that city in 1980. The model had no great deductive logic, but embodied a considerable number of *ad hoc* judgments at critical points. Nor had it any great statistical sophistication. The area under study was broken up into small subdivisions. Then for each of these the future pattern of land uses was extrapolated according to a series of rules which were drawn up for each of six types of land use: residential, commercial, manufacturing, transportation, public buildings and public open-space. The detailed rules need not be spelt out here: it is sufficient to record that the forecast was based on the land-use inventory in a particular sub-district, on its zoning map and on its location within the city. The future land use for each subdistrict was then projected separately; and although there was some attempt to see that the land-use totals for the whole city made some over-all sense, the model paid little attention to the general operation of the urban land market, which of course transcends the sub-district boundaries.

This CATS model may be criticized because its use of theory is weak and because much depends on personal judgments by the research staff on the future land-use changes that would take place. On the other hand it represented a reasonably good strategy for making effective "rule-of-thumb" decisions for the practical purpose of transportation planning, at a time when more advanced methods were unavailable, particularly as it was backed by a good knowledge of local conditions. Certainly this kind of approach has little academic appeal since its value is specific to a particular city and it makes no pretension to theoretical sophistication. It merely attempts to make an informed statement about what the future land-use map will be like if certain current trends are continued; and these results then form a basis for transport planning proposals which would make such a future land-use pattern function with the minimum of economic friction. There is, of course, the possibility that current trends will alter, particularly if considerable changes are made to the capacity and form of the transportation network; but this same difficulty also applies to later, more advanced transportation models that followed the pioneer work in Chicago.

A contrasting example of an urban model is provided by the work of the Center for Urban and Regional Studies at the University of North Carolina. Here attention was focused on residential land use and the general purpose of the model was to predict the conversion of rural land to residential purposes as the urban population increased. The area under study was divided into small cells, each of which was given an index of attractiveness for residential development, based on factors like accessibility to employment, sewage facilities, schools and major highways. It was assumed that the probability of residential development was proportional to a cell's attractiveness; and in predicting the form of residential development the cells in which development was assumed to take place were chosen by random sampling, with allowance being made for the varying levels of probability that particular cells would be chosen for residential building at successive stages in urban growth. The random element in this model was designed to allow for the chance considerations that often interfere with the decisions being made by developers, although the actual process of decision-making was not explicitly included in the model. This approach recognizes that not all areas are equally attractive for urban development; and the measure of attractiveness may be seen as an indirect indication of the operation of the market for urban residential land. It must be noted, however, that the model only partially simulates the provision of homes, since it only represents the conversion of rural land to residential purposes and makes no allowance for the redevelopment that occurs within already built-up areas. As a predictive device, too, the model is dependent on the availability of accurate population projections which are always difficult to provide for small areas. It is also a model that can be most easily applied in societies where there is a relatively free market in land.

A third example, and possibly the most widely-applied urban growth model so far produced, was devised by I. S. Lowry as part of a study of the Pittsburg region. In essence this model combined two earlier statements about distributional patterns within cities with a simple interpretation of the urban economic base. One of these statements was to do with the relationship between place of employment and place of residence and was developed from ideas about population density gradients within cities, with residential densities being assumed to fall away in a logical manner around centres of employment. The second underlying assumption was concerned with the distribution of service employment likely to occur in relation to the general distribution of residential population. This was developed from Reilly's law of retail gravitation and assumed that the location and employment levels of the service sector were strongly influenced by accessibility to local final customers, whose effect was progressively reduced the farther away they lived.

The Lowry model linked these two ideas by using the concept that a basic and non-basic sector could be identified in the urban economic base and by following a relatively simple procedure. The location of basic employment was taken as given and was allocated to various predetermined locations within the area under study, which was sub-divided into zones. Then the population distribution that was likely to be associated with that employment was calculated, with assumptions being made about the total housing stock that could be expected in each zone and with the effect of a particular employment centre being allowed to spread over to other zones. Service employment was then allocated in relation to the distribution of residential population that had already been forecast. As the addition of the non-basic employment implied further residential population the model was then run again to allocate the homes of these additional workers and the service employment which, in turn, was associated with them. As a result further runs of the model were required; and this procedure was repeated until no important additions of non-basic population became apparent.

The Lowry model remains an ingenious piece of work, but it is not without its own particular difficulties. In practice the distinction between basic and non-basic employment is not always easy to make. The model suppresses all questions to do with land-use succession within different parts of a city, and the migration of activities within a city is also not considered. There is no attempt to disaggregate the behaviour of different socio-economic groups, which could well be relevant for the journey to work and for the growth of socially-distinctive residential areas. Nevertheless the model has been widely adopted, and attempts have been made to modify it for conditions outside the United States: for example, at least two pieces of planning research in Britain have taken the Lowry model as their starting point.

There are two reasons for this. First, the model is relatively easy to apply to particular planning problems, provided that its underlying assumptions are acceptable. For example, various amounts of future basic employment can be postulated and then their effects on the form of the city can be explored. Or again, planning decisions (like the prevention of residential building on particular tracts of land) can be built in and the probable results of these policies on the total urban pattern can be observed. Second, although the underlying assumptions in the model are not elaborate, at least it has theoretical underpinning from a number of aspects of urban geography. The fact that the resulting model is a hybrid of three general observations drawn from urban geography at least reflects something of the reality of urban life, which cannot be embraced by any single over-riding theory.

Various other models of urban development have been devised. Some are statistically much more elaborate, but all of them have in common the aim of projecting some aspects of the city of the future. Some important general comments arise.

First it should be recalled that, by and large, models of urban development are based on the current processes that are operating within the western city. Not only may they not be appropriate in other culture realms, but they may also not be relevant in the western world itself at some future time. Some attempt can be made to devise models which include likely future developments, but their basic assumptions are firmly rooted in the present. Most models assume that the aspirations of society, the functioning of the urban economy and the underlying technical basis of urban life will stay constant. Unfortunately these are assumptions that are particularly suspect in the rapidly changing modern world. It follows that the predictions that are made on the basis of these models are more useful over the short-term, rather than over longer periods. Long-term predictions produce dramatic results, but short-term indications are much more reliable and valuable.

There is also a very real danger that the forecasts provided by these models will be self-fulfilling. If plans are made to accommodate the results that the models predict, for example by the provision of appropriate transport facilities, then these very decisions will produce strong forces encouraging the creation of the city as forecast, rather than the city that it might be desirable to live in at some future time.

At best, too, urban development models can only provide a partial and simplified view of urban life, but it is important to recall that in fact urban growth consists of a complex combination of decisions by developers and occupiers to build and to buy, to move and to expand, to develop and to preserve from change, all these decisions being taken in the context of various social, legal and financial constraints. Although there may be superficial similarities, urban development is not a process like the spread of an ice-cap or the growth of a fungus over a piece of cheese. Such analogies may have some descriptive usefulness, but in the last resort they represent fundamentally different processes from the aggregation of human decisions involved in urban expansion.

As urban development need not be a mechanistic process it is appropriate for society itself to specify the kind of city that would be a suitable place in which to live, and then to make planning decisions that are likely to produce an appropriate result. The models of urban development that are currently being elaborated have an important part to play in the appraisal of the probable effects of these decisions, but they have only a limited role in the intellectual process of specifying goals for the designer of the future city. There remain many aesthetic and social judgments with which the models cannot help, but which are inescapable in producing a city that will be aesthetically and socially acceptable as well as economically viable.

Selected Reading

E. W. Burgess published his Concentric theory in 1924, but the article was reprinted and made more widely known in

R. E. PARK, E. W. BURGESS and R. D. McKENZIE, *The City* (Chicago, 1925), pp. 47–62.

This and other theories of urban structure are examined in

A. H. HAWLEY, *Human Ecology: a Theory of Community Structure* (New York, 1950), chapter 14, Spatial aspects of ecological organization.

Davie's theory of urban structure is found in

M. R. DAVIE, The pattern of urban growth, in G. P. Murdock (ed.), *Studies in the Science of Society* (New Haven, 1937), pp. 133–61.

Hoyt's sector theory appeared two years later in

H. HOYT, *The Structure and Growth of Residential Neighbourhoods in American Cities* (Washington, 1939);

but the basic ideas of the outward migration of "high rent" areas appear in

H. Hoyt, *One Hundred Years of Land Values in Chicago* (Chicago, 1933).

New data on the distribution of income groups in modern United States' cities are analysed in

H. Hoyt, *Where the Rich and Poor People Live* (Technical Bulletin no. 55, Urban Land Institute, Washington, 1966).

The sector and concentric ideas are combined in a "model" of a typical British city in

P. Mann, *An Approach to Urban Sociology* (London, 1965), chapter 4, Urban society.

The role of social forces in shaping urban land use is explored in

W. Firey, *Land Use in Central Boston* (Cambridge, Mass., 1947).

The Multiple Nuclei theory is advanced in

C. D. Harris and E. L. Ullman, The nature of cities, *Annals of the American Academy of Political and Social Science* **242** (1945), 7–17. [Reprinted in H. M. Mayer and C. F. Kohn, *Readings in Urban Geography* (Chicago, 1959), pp. 277–86.]

Early attempts at gradient analysis include

E. W. Burgess, The determination of gradients in the growth of the city, *Proceedings of the American Sociological Society* **21** (1927), 178–84.
C. R. Shaw et al., *Delinquency Areas* (Chicago, 1929).

A classic paper by a geographer which explored similar territory is

C. C. Colby, Centrifugal and centripetal forces in urban geography, *Annals of the Association of American Geographers* **23** (1933), 1–20.

A descriptive study which shook the easy generalization of the Concentric theory of urban structure is

C. D. Harris, Suburbs, *American Journal of Sociology* **49** (1943), 1–13.

A recent survey of the literature in this field, with suggestions for a new approach, is

E. Gittus, The structure of urban areas: a new approach, *Town Planning Review* **35** (1964), 5–20.

The thesis that the pre-industrial city forms a distinct urban type is presented in

G. Sjoberg, *The Pre-industrial City: Past and Present* (Glencoe, Illinois, 1960).

For a critique of this idea see

P. Wheatley, "What the greatness of a city is said to be": reflections on Sjoberg's "Pre-industrial City", *Pacific Viewpoint* **4** (1965), 163–88.

An example of the dual structure of a former colonial town is given in

A. Mabogunje, The growth of the residential districts in Ibadan, *Geographical Review* **52** (1962), 56–77.

A useful summary and commentary on current urban development models is

Highway Research Board, *Urban Development Models* (Special Report no. 97, Washington, 1968).

On the CATS model see

J. R. Hamburg and R. H. Sharkey, *Land Use Forecast* (Chicago Area Transportation Study, Chicago, 1961).

Some aspects of the findings of the Center for Urban and Regional Studies of the University of North Carolina are discussed in

F. STUART CHAPIN, Jr., A model for simulating residential development, *Journal of the American Institute of Planners* **31** (1965), 120–5.

A discussion of the Lowry model and some aspects of its application are explored in

D. B. MASSEY and M. CORDEY-HAYES, The use of models in structure planning, *Town Planning Review* **42** (1971), 28–44.

See also,

M. ECHENIQUE, D. CROWTHER and W. LINDSAY, A spatial model of urban stock and activity, *Regional Studies* **3** (1969), 281–312.

A NOTE ON FURTHER READING

WORK on urban geography has been scattered in many different learned periodicals, so that a number of collections of journal articles, reprinted as single volumes, provide particularly convenient sources for further reading.

An interesting collection of articles, which largely reflects American work up to the mid-1950's, is

H. M. MAYER and C. F. KOHN (eds.), *Readings in Urban Geography* (Chicago, 1959).

More recent geographical writing is included in

L. S. BOURNE (ed.), *Internal Structure of the City: Readings on Space and Environment* (New York, 1971).

Many aspects of urban geography are integrated into the general field of human geography in

P. HAGGETT, *Locational Analysis in Human Geography* (London, 1965).

Social aspects of urban life are covered by

E. W. BURGESS and D. J. BOGUE (eds.), *Contributions to Urban Sociology* (Chicago, 1964); and
G. A. THEODORSON (ed.), *Studies in Human Ecology* (Evanston, 1961).

A particularly wide-ranging collection of reprinted articles, largely with a socio-logical bias is

S. F. FAVA (ed.), *Urbanism in World Perspective: a Reader* (New York, 1968).

A collection of articles which also contains some interest for the urban geographer is

J. FRIEDMANN and W. ALONSO, *Regional Development and Planning: a Reader* (Cambridge, Mass., 1964);

and on a specialist economic problem see

R. W. PFOUTS (ed.), *The Techniques of Urban Economic Analysis* (New York, 1960).

The economic background of other aspects of urban life is summarized in a collection of reprinted articles:

W. H. LEAHY, D. L. McKEE and R. D. DEAN (eds.), *Urban Economics: Theory, Development and Planning* (New York, 1970).

A recent collection of original articles which contains European as well as American contributions is

K. NORBORG (ed.), *Proceedings of the I.G.U. Symposium on Urban Geography, Lund 1960* (Lund, 1962).

A popular account of current urban problems is given by the collection of essays in
Scientific American **213**, no. 3 (Sept., 1965), also published in book form as

Cities—*a Scientific American Book* (New York, 1965).

For an extensive bibliography, which covers many of the relevant journal articles,
published before about 1950, see

P. SCHÖLLER, Aufgabe und Probleme der Stadtgeographie, *Erdkunde* **7** (1953),
161–84.

For a comprehensive survey of more recent literature, particularly that published in
English and covering other disciplines as well as geography, see

P. M. HAUSER and L. F. SCHNORE (eds.), *The Study of Urbanization* (New York,
1965).

Each year, of course, brings important new additions to the literature, and current
periodicals should be examined for relevant material. In Britain, besides the conventional geographical periodicals, the *Town Planning Review* is an important source
of articles of great interest to the urban geographer. So, too, is *Urban Studies* and four
other planning journals—*Town and Country Planning, Journal of the Town Planning
Institute, Planning Outlook* and *Regional Studies*. Urban geography plays an important
part in American geographical writing, so that the three leading geographical
periodicals in the U.S.A.—*Annals of the Association of American Geographers, Geographical
Review* and *Economic Geography*—contain many articles of interest. The *Papers and
Proceedings of the Regional Science Association* and the *Journal of Regional Science* also contain many articles of value to the urban geographer.

INDEX

199